Securing SAP® S/4HANA

Christophe Decamps,
Bert Vanstechelman,
Chris Walravens

Thank you for purchasing this book from Espresso Tutorials!

Like a cup of espresso coffee, Espresso Tutorials SAP books are concise and effective. We know that your time is valuable and we deliver information in a succinct and straightforward manner. It only takes our readers a short amount of time to consume SAP concepts. Our books are well recognized in the industry for leveraging tutorial-style instruction and videos to show you step by step how to successfully work with SAP.

Check out our YouTube channel to watch our videos at
https://www.youtube.com/user/EspressoTutorials.

If you are interested in SAP Finance and Controlling, join us at
http://www.fico-forum.com/forum2/
to get your SAP questions answered and contribute to discussions.

Related titles from Espresso Tutorials:

- Tracy Juran: Beginner's Guide to SAP® Security and Authorizations
  http://5013.espresso-tutorials.com
- Christian Savelli: SAP® BW on SAP HANA
  http://5128.espresso-tutorials.com
- Janet Salmon & Claus Wild: First Steps in SAP® S/4HANA Finance
  http://5149.espresso-tutorials.com
- Raquel Seville: SAP® OpenUI5 for Mobile BI and Analytics
  http://5173.espresso-tutorials.com
- Robert Burdwell: First Steps for Building SAP®UI5 Mobile Apps
  http://5176.espresso-tutorials.com
- Frank Riesner, Klaus-Peter Sauer: SAP BW/4HANA and BW on HANA
  http://5215.espresso-tutorials.com
- Maxim Chuprunov: Leveraging SAP® GRC in the Fight Against Corruption and Fraud
  http://5216.espresso-tutorials.com
- Bert Vanstechelman: The SAP® HANA Implementation Guide
  http://5289.espresso-tutorials.com

Christophe Decamps, Bert Vanstechelman, Chris Walravens
Securing SAP® S/4HANA

ISBN:	978-3-96012-249-4
Editor:	Tracey Duffy
Cover Design:	Philip Esch
Cover Photo:	© psdesign1 # 152111897 – stock.adobe.com
Interior Book Design:	Johann-Christian Hanke

1st Edition 2018

URL: *www.espresso-tutorials.com*

Feedback
We greatly appreciate any feedback you may have concerning this book. Please send your feedback via email to: *info@espresso-tutorials.com*.

Table of Contents

Introduction

SAP S/4HANA is the latest version of the ERP suite available from SAP. It represents the fourth major technology change in the SAP ERP suite. For this version, SAP has rewritten the original ABAP code to use the full power of the HANA database. In this book, we focus on how these major changes impact how you set up roles and authorizations in your S/4HANA landscape.

In 1979, SAP launched its first ERP package—called SAP R/2. This software package combined several business processes (including finance and materials management) in one application and included data storage on a central database. SAP R/2 was based on mainframe technology. Combining several business tasks into one package represented a first major technology shift in business applications. From a security perspective, creating authorization profiles was primarily a manual activity at that time.

In the early 1990s, SAP moved to client-server technology with the release of SAP R/3. With regard to authorizations, the SAP R/3 releases also introduced the now well-known Profile Generator (PFCG), which largely automated the creation of authorization profiles.

By 2004, SAP had introduced its SAP ERP Central Component (ECC) release, allowing customers to transition towards service-oriented architectures and towards Internet integration. The most recent version is SAP ECC 6.0 Enhancement Package 8, which was released in 2016.

SAP S/4HANA is the fourth major technology change in the ERP software offered by SAP. While the previous releases were designed to run on various databases (provided by other vendors such as Oracle), the S/4HANA suite now runs on SAP's proprietary in-memory database platform SAP HANA. With this move, SAP is following the current major trend of in-memory computing and big data applications. It is also getting rid of one of its major frustrations: the need for external database providers, especially its old rival Oracle. The full suite, from the front end, through the application layer, to the database platform, is now provided by SAP itself.

S/4HANA is a game changer when it comes to setting up security. Up to the ECC releases, the main security concern for logical access was the back-end system itself. The traditional front-end applications (SAP GUI, NetWeaver Business Client) did not require an extensive (if any) security setup. The underlying database for ECC did not require complex security either because the database layer was accessed by only a few people and it was mainly the ECC application that communicated with the database. With S/4HANA, this all changes:

- The S/4HANA back-end security mechanisms remain but the security setup is more complex because the traditional security, based on transaction codes, is increasingly complemented by UI5 applications.
- The new Fiori front end also requires a security setup to ensure the end user is presented with a highly personalized set of tiles. Not implementing tile roles of the appropriate quality on the front end will significantly reduce the user experience and will make the consistent link with the back-end roles difficult.
- The HANA platform is much more than just a database. The power of HANA will be increasingly exploited through native HANA applications consuming data directly from the HANA database. You will therefore have to set up adequate HANA roles, ideally applying the same security concept and the same restriction requirements to HANA that you apply to the S/4HANA application, even though the security mechanisms of HANA and S/4HANA are fundamentally different.

This book will introduce you to the specific security mechanisms on the different systems involved: the S/4HANA application, the SAP NetWeaver Gateway system, and the HANA database platform. Furthermore, we will provide ideas and concepts for creating a consistent cross-system authorization concept, translating the technical specifics of each system into an overall consistent security model. In addition to the aspects of logical access control, we will also look at the technical security aspects of S/4HANA.

We start our adventure in Chapter 1, where we focus on securing the S/4HANA application and compare it to the existing SAP ERP security model. What has changed and what has not? We provide insights into the technical aspects of setting up S/4HANA authorizations, the impact of the new front end, the database security setup, and the need to make those different levels consistent with one another.

In Chapter 2, we dive into SAP Fiori, which is the new user experience (UX) for SAP software and applications. It provides a set of applications that are used in regular business functions such as work approvals, financial apps, calculation apps, and various self-service apps.

After discussing the S/4HANA and Fiori security in the previous chapters, in Chapter 3, we focus on security for the HANA database. As SAP HANA allows you to work directly in the database when modeling or consuming views, security has to be considered not only from the application layer point of view but also from the database point of view.

Finally, in Chapter 4, we focus on securing the SAP application server, the database, the operating system, and the network infrastructure.

Acknowledgments

This book is built on the many years of experience of the three authors and so we really should acknowledge everybody who has contributed to enabling us to acquire that experience over the years. We should probably also be thanking one another: each of us has learned many things from the others. Our gratitude also goes to our colleagues at Expertum, especially Tom Lanssens for proofreading the chapters. We are a fast-growing company and have more than a century of combined SAP experience between us. Our reference list of SAP implementation projects is breathtaking. Finally, and most importantly, I must thank my wife, Ilka, for supporting me in writing yet another book. Chris would like to thank his girlfriend, Virginie, for indulging his writing during the strangest of hours. Christophe thanks his wife, Roxane, and his children, Lorentz and Lazlo, for their support and patience.

Our most sincere thanks also go to Alice Adams of Espresso Tutorials for her advice and support and to Tracey Duffy, who edited the manuscript until it was perfect.

We have added a few icons to highlight important information. These include:

Tips

Tips highlight information that provides more details about the subject being described and/or additional background information.

Attention

Attention notices highlight information that you should be aware of when you go through the examples in this book on your own.

Finally, a note concerning the copyright: all screenshots printed in this book are the copyright of SAP SE. All rights are reserved by SAP SE. Copyright pertains to all SAP images in this publication. For the sake of simplicity, we do not mention this specifically underneath every screenshot.

1 Securing S/4HANA

In this chapter, we focus on securing the S/4HANA application layer, the counterpart of the traditional ECC security. What has changed? What remains unchanged? We provide insights into the technical aspects of setting up S/4HANA authorizations. We also provide insights into the conceptual considerations, which have changed drastically, by introducing the front-end and database security setup required and especially the need to make these three levels (front-end security, back-end security, database platform security) consistent with one another.

1.1 Generic steps for back-end roles

Let us start with some good news: although the front-end and database technology is changing drastically (refer to the subsequent chapters in this book to learn about the security implications of these new aspects), and although SAP is rewriting its ABAP code to optimize it for SAP HANA, the mechanisms for securing the S/4HANA back-end functionality remain largely intact. In this section, we will focus on the generic steps needed to secure the S/4HANA application layer. You will notice that many aspects and the best practices that we have become familiar with over the years are still applicable.

1.1.1 Grouping transaction codes into single roles

Whatever role concept you have created in the past (we will look at the conceptual options in more detail in Section 1.3), one of the essential steps has always been the grouping of transaction codes into single roles. To grant access to transaction codes, you have to group them into single roles in some way. This applies to the SAP standard transaction codes a company uses in its business processes as well as to the custom-developed transaction codes a company creates to enhance the standard SAP functionality. The authorization objects included in the ABAP code of these transaction codes (often forgotten in programs developed in-house) also have to be included in these single roles with the required and correct field values.

Does this change in S/4HANA? No, not at all. In particular, in scenarios where only a few specific Fiori apps are used in combination with the traditional SAP GUI and/or SAP Business Client as the front end, SAP authorization roles still have to be created in the old-fashioned way. Users will still need access to the back-end transaction codes in the same way as before.

1.1.2 Integrating field restrictions

Granting access to transaction codes has always been only part of the authorizations story. In most cases, further restrictions are required within the transaction codes. These restrictions can be divided into three types:

Activity-like restrictions

Although some transaction codes are used solely to create, change, or display data, for other transaction codes, it is the authorizations at object level that determine whether a transaction code is accessible in create, change, or display mode. For example, transaction code ME21N is used specifically for creating purchase orders. This transaction code itself does nothing but allow the user to create purchase orders. In contrast, transaction code OB52 is used to open and close posting periods in accounting. It is the underlying object S_TABU_DIS (or S_TABU_NAM) that determines whether you can access the underlying data in change mode (ACTVT = 02 on the object) or only in display mode (ACTVT = 03 on the object). This type of restriction will become even more important in a Fiori app setting because we predict that Fiori apps will focus on a set of data or a process. The mode in which the user has access to the data or process will be determined by the security at field level. Unlike the traditional transaction codes, we predict that the new UI5 Fiori apps will not be duplicated to provide create, change, and display variants. This kind of restriction has to be implemented at the level of single roles.

Organizational restrictions

The SAP system traditionally comes with organizational levels in the *Profile Generator (PFCG)*. These authorization object fields have a special status, allowing them to be maintained centrally within each role. This means that when such a field appears in multiple authorization objects within a role, the field values only have to be maintained once within the role. These values are then propagated throughout the role. Classic organizational levels are COMPANY CODE (BUKRS), PLANT (WERKS), PURCHASING ORGANIZATION (EKORG), SALES ORGANIZATION (VKORG), etc. It is very common for a company to need restrictions on a combination of these organizational levels. In S/4HANA, this principle and mechanism remains untouched: PFCG still includes working with organizational levels within the roles. Organizational restrictions are always translated into derived roles: the transaction codes and other field level restrictions are inherited from the imparting roles. Derived roles only differ from their parent in terms of the organizational restrictions.

Functional restrictions

All other, non-organizational fields can still be used to implement further restrictions within the transaction codes. Classical examples of such fields are MOVEMENT TYPE (BWART), INFOTYPE (INFTY), PURCHASING DOCUMENT TYPE (BSART), BILLING TYPE (FKART), etc. Different sets of functional restrictions have to be translated into different single roles. For example, if there are two types of purchase orders and these two types are used in different purchasing flows (and different users have access to these purchasing document types), then two distinct single roles have to be created, giving access to the separate document types respectively.

It is reassuring to know that although the database table structure has changed drastically in S/4HANA, the well-known authorization objects and restriction options these objects provide still apply. SAP has not made any fundamental changes to the authorization objects that are available and have been checked. Of course, as with every upgrade to a new release in the past, some objects have become obsolete and others have been added, but the change is not fundamental. These changes can be treated just like a traditional upgrade.

It was and still is good practice to document all the required and applicable restrictions in an *authorization restriction grid (ARG)*. This type of central restriction document (see Figure 1.1) contains the following elements:

- All authorization object fields on which a restriction is required: the fields listed in this document are all covered by a business requirement to have a restriction on them. The implication is that if an object field is not listed in the document, the field can be ignored from the perspective of restrictions.
- The different restriction domains: a specific set of restriction values is grouped into a *restriction domain*. This domain must be coded such that it can be used and translated into derived roles. Typical examples of domains are: regions, countries, legal entities (company codes), sites, plants, sales areas, etc.
- The applicable values per field/domain combination.

				2	2	3	4	5
		Restriction Field	Restriction Field Description	INFR_XXXX	9200_9200	9210_XXXX	9216_9216	9250_XXXX
		BUKRS	Company Code	9*	9200	9210	9216	9250
		FCLM_BUKRS	Company Code	9*	9200	9210	9216	9250
	FI	RCOMP	Company Code	9*	9200	9210	9216	9250
		BWKEY	Valuation Area	9*	9200	9210, 9220, 9240	9216	9250, 9251, 9255, 9260
		KTOPL	Chart of Accounts	RS01	RS01	RS01	RS01	RS01
		KOKRS	Controlling Area	S001	S001	S001	S001	S001
		FCLM_KOKRS	Controlling Area	S001	S001	S001	S001	S001
S	CO	KOSTL	Cost Center	*	*	*	*	*
		PRCTR	Profit Center	09*	09200*	09210*, 09220*, 09240*	09216*	09250*, 09251*, 09255*, 09260*
4		FCLM_PRCTR	Profit Center	09*	09200*	09210*, 09220*, 09240*	09216*	09250*, 09251*, 09255*, 09260*
H	PS	/CPD/MP_OR	Service Organization	9*, ' '	9200*, ' '	9210*, 9220*, 9220*, 9240*, ' '	9216*, ' '	9250*, 9251*, 9255*, 9260*, ' '
A		WERKS	Plant	9*	9200	9210, 9220, 9240	9216	9250, 9251, 9255, 9260
	MM	EKORG	Purchasing Organization	9*	9000	9000	9000	9000
		EKGRP	Purchasing Group	*	*	*	*	*
N		KLAGR	Class Group	ETM	ETM	ETM	ETM	ETM
	PP	CSWRK	Plant	9*	9200	9210, 9220, 9240	9216	9250, 9251, 9255, 9260
A	PM	IWERK	Maintenance Planning Plant	9*	9200	9210, 9220, 9240	9216	9250, 9251, 9255, 9260
		SWERK	Maintenance plant	9*	9200	9210, 9220, 9240	9216	9250, 9251, 9255, 9260
		VKORG	Sales Organization	9*	9200	9210, 9220, 9240	9216	9250, 9251, 9255, 9260
	SD	VTWEG	Distribution Channel	10, 20	10, 20	10	20	10, 20
		SPART	Division	10, 20	10, 20	10	20	10, 20
		VSTEL	Shipping Point	*	*	*	*	*
	HR	PERSA	Personnel Area	9*	9200	9210, 9220, 9220, 9240	9216	9250, 9251, 9255, 9260
		VDSK1	Organisational Key					

Figure 1.1: Example of an authorization restriction grid (ARG) document

From a change management perspective, the authorization restriction grid document should be used as a conceptual document that has to be updated first before changes to the role content are implemented. We strongly believe that this is the only way to ensure that every change is made with the big picture in mind. In particular, when using group domains (grouping several company codes or plants, for example), updating the authorization restriction grid first ensures that the updates are implemented in the correct domains and in all domains necessary. It also ensures that the content of the roles remains consistent for each domain. Finally, this type of central document also allows regular and automated technical updates to and monitoring of the role content, again ensuring the role content remains aligned with the documentation (the documentation being the actual business requirements).

1.1.3 Grouping user access into composite roles

While creating single roles is inevitable, and creating derived roles is strongly recommended for organizational restrictions when you are setting up SAP logical access security, the use of composite roles is optional to a certain extent. Creating, maintaining, and using composite roles remains identical in S/4HANA compared to SAP ECC. Refer to Section 1.3.3 for a more conceptual discussion on how to use composite roles.

1.1.4 Identifying access to be monitored

To grant access to an SAP system, you have to create roles and assign them to users. These roles, as explained in the previous sections, contain the required authorizations for executing transaction codes, programs, WebDynpros, and Fiori apps. When you assign roles to users, the generated profiles from the roles are automatically assigned to the users as well. This mechanism is straightforward. However, the difficulty and complexity in SAP authorizations emerges when multiple roles and profiles are assigned to a user. Let's look at the technical details of this aspect.

When a user logs on to an SAP system, what happens technically is that the user buffer is filled with individual authorizations. The SAP system runs through all individually assigned profiles of the user and builds a flat list of individual authorizations—the user buffer. So far, so good.

When a user executes a certain transaction code or Fiori app, the SAP system performs built-in authority checks to decide the further flow of the program. These authority checks can be triggered in the kernel (S_TCODE, S_SERVICE), they can be triggered from the transaction code definition (transaction code SE93), they can come from within ABAP code, etc. Whenever such an authority check is performed, the SAP system compares the required values with the authorizations available in the user buffer. The SAP system only continues to the next authority check when a suitable authorization is found in the user buffer. The user can only complete their task once all authority checks for the functionality have been completed successfully. In all other cases, the user receives a message such as YOU ARE NOT AUTHORIZED..., thereby preventing them from doing what they are trying to do.

It is important to note that once the user is logged on, the way the roles are created is irrelevant. It is solely the content of the user buffer that determines whether a user has access to a certain functionality or not. Therefore, regardless of how crucial the role structure is for creating, maintaining, approving, and providing access to your SAP system, once a user has logged on, it is the flat list of authorizations in the user buffer that determines everything.

This is where the potential accumulation of access rights comes in. Take a simple example of two roles assigned to a user. In an SAP system, it is very feasible that each role gives **full and complete** access to **just one** piece of functionality, whilst also containing some authorizations for another piece of functionality—for example, role 1 gives full and complete access only to functionality A, and role 2 gives full and complete access only to functionality B. However, assigning both roles to one user, and thus combining the authorizations of both roles into one user buffer, might grant access to more than functionality A + B! This is because (in this example) role 1 contains all the required authorizations for functionality A and some of the authorizations for functionality C. If you assign only role 1, only functionality A is accessible. Role 2 in our example contains all the required authorizations for functionality B, together with the missing authorizations for functionality C. Again, assigning only role 2 makes only functionality B available. Combining role 1 and 2 grants access to functionality C as well, as the combination means that all required authorizations for functionality C are present. Imagine the complexity of this potential mechanism when hundreds of roles are assigned to a user—a scenario that is very common.

This again proves how essential a strong authorizations concept is for guaranteeing that the accumulation of access rights is reduced to a minimum. However, regardless of how good and strong your authorizations concept is, because of the sheer complexity of the mechanism described, you will still need a strong monitoring procedure.

To monitor authorizations, you need the following:

- A list of (combinations of) functionality that your company considers as being a risk when not controlled adequately. When executing an authorizations implementation project, for efficiency purposes, it makes sense to also include this list of functionality to be monitored in the implementation scope. Indeed, when executing the implementation, you have to look at the business processes anyway. Therefore, considering the risk aspect at the same time is usually very efficient. One case where this is especially true is when considering transaction codes developed in-house: these have to be assigned to single roles anyway, which often requires extensive investigation into what exactly each transaction code developed in-house does. Including the aspect of making a transaction code ruleset relevant often requires only a little more effort in the overall analysis.
- An application containing a risk engine capable of running risk analyses, providing root cause analysis, and delivering dashboard reporting.
- A detailed ruleset which translates the functionality to be monitored into technical queries to be used in the analysis engine. This analysis engine must work in the same way as the user buffer mechanism described. It is not sufficient to monitor only certain role assignments, nor is it sufficient to monitor only access to transaction codes. The analysis mechanism must work in the same way as the SAP authority checks: traditionally, this is a combination of an S_TCODE authorization together with authorizations on some key objects with specific activity-like values.

One leading application on the market that meets all the requirements is SAP's own *SAP Access Control*. This application contains all the required monitoring functionality. The ruleset structure used in SAP Access Control is a good example of how a ruleset should be constructed.

As you can see in Figure 1.2, a ruleset consists of the following elements:

- *Functions*: these are the detailed queries for evaluating whether a user has access to certain functionality. They consist of *actions* (the equivalent of transaction codes) and *permissions* (the equivalent of authorizations).
- *Risks*: these consist of one to a maximum of five functions. It is the risk level that the application uses to run its analysis against.
- *Rulesets*: these group risks together. Risks can be combined/reused in one or more rulesets.

The following types of risks are available:

- *Critical access*: technically, only one function is selected in this type of risk. From a monitoring perspective, this means that a certain piece of functionality is monitored by itself—for example, who can open and close posting periods.
- *Segregation of duties (SoD)*: technically, at least two (and up to five) functions are selected in this type of risk. The segregation of duties risk thus monitors combinations of functionality—the classical SoD conflicts.
- *Critical permissions*: these risks are like the critical access risks but the selected functions contain only permissions and no actions. A classic example of this type of function/risk is access to debugging mode in the SAP system: no S_TCODE authorization is required for accessing debug mode, only some specific (S_DEVELOP) authorizations. To monitor this type of access, the critical permission type of risk is required.

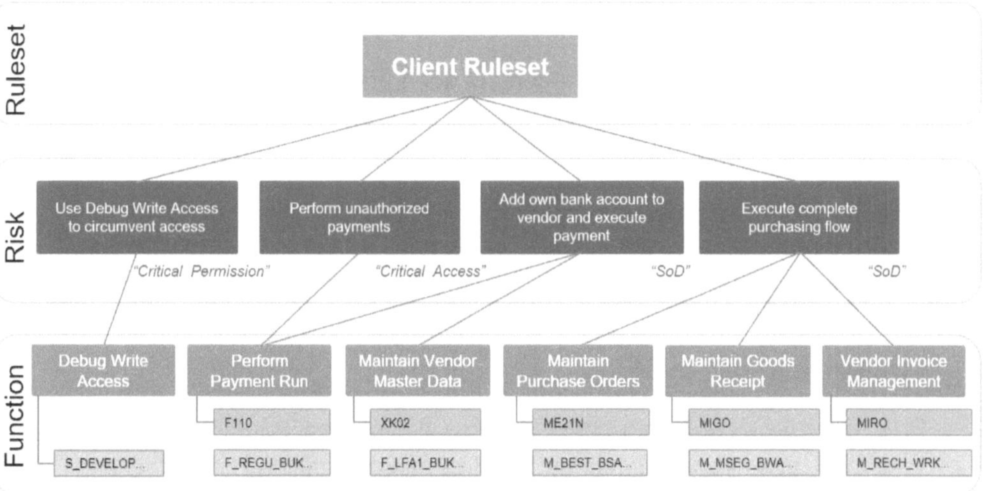

Figure 1.2: Building blocks for an SAP authorizations ruleset

1.1.5 Implementing roles in the system

As already stated, there are no fundamental changes in the way back-end authorization roles are created and maintained. In particular, in the scenario where Fiori apps are used only for specific purposes, most of the S4/HANA functionality remains accessible via the traditional user interfaces (SAP GUI, SAP Business Client). In this case, the well-known techniques for building roles using the Profile Generator (PFCG) remain intact. It is only when Fiori starts to be used extensively that there is a slight change in approach. We will discuss this in Section 1.2.

Because the way of working on the back-end system remains largely the same as in the previous SAP releases, we will only mention a few elements here that we consider important when administering SAP back-end roles:

Change management

Always apply the change management good practices. Create and maintain roles in a development system (typically, the ideal environment for this is the customizing *golden client*), transport the changes to a quality assurance system to allow testing in a stable environment, and transport the tested and approved changes to the productive client. Although this might seem obvious, we still see companies not (fully) complying with this way of working.

Transaction code SU24

Use the Profile Generator (PFCG) to its full extent. This statement largely refers to using transaction code SU24 to maintain tables USOBX_C and USOBT_C optimally. These two tables form the heart of the Profile Generator. SAP has taken the effort to document all the authority checks in the SAP standard tables USOBX and USOBT. Table USOBX contains all objects for each transaction code that will be automatically pulled into a single role by PFCG whenever a given transaction code is added to the role menu. Table USOBT contains the default field values that are automatically pulled in. When you activate PFCG, the system creates customer-specific copies of these SAP standard tables by adding *_C* to the name of the tables. Using transaction code SU24 to maintain your custom values is strongly recommended. A classic example of this is the custom-developed transaction code, for which it is strongly advisable to document the authority checks in transaction SU24 (see Figure 1.3 for an example).

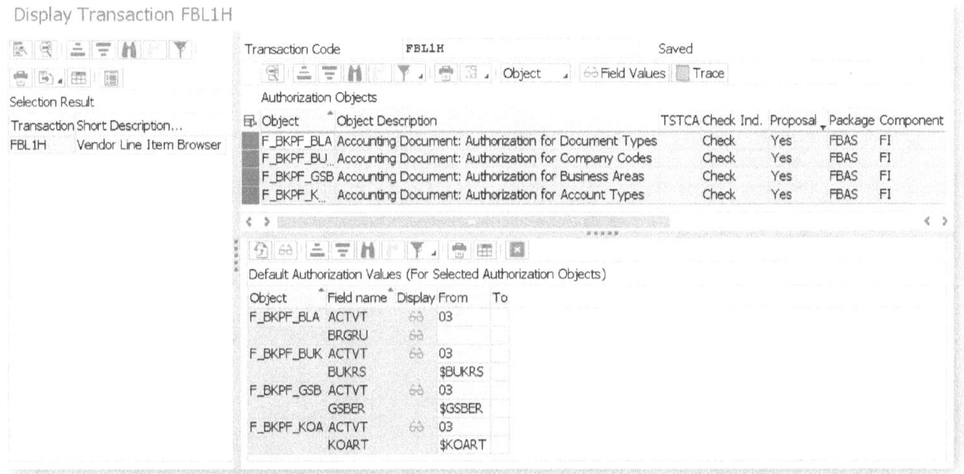

Figure 1.3: Example of SU24 data for transaction code FBL1H

Transaction code SU25

Strongly related to the previous point, run transaction code SU25 every time you implement a *Support Package (SP)* or upgrade. Indeed, with every SP and upgrade, the SAP system receives new authorization objects, new checks on existing objects, etc. These are not automatically reflected in your customer _C tables. Running transaction code SU25 will update your customer tables without touching the specific customer values maintained through transaction code SU24. The SU25 process described is required in particular if you upgrade your current ECC authorization concept to S/4HANA. See Figure 1.4 for the screen for transaction SU25.

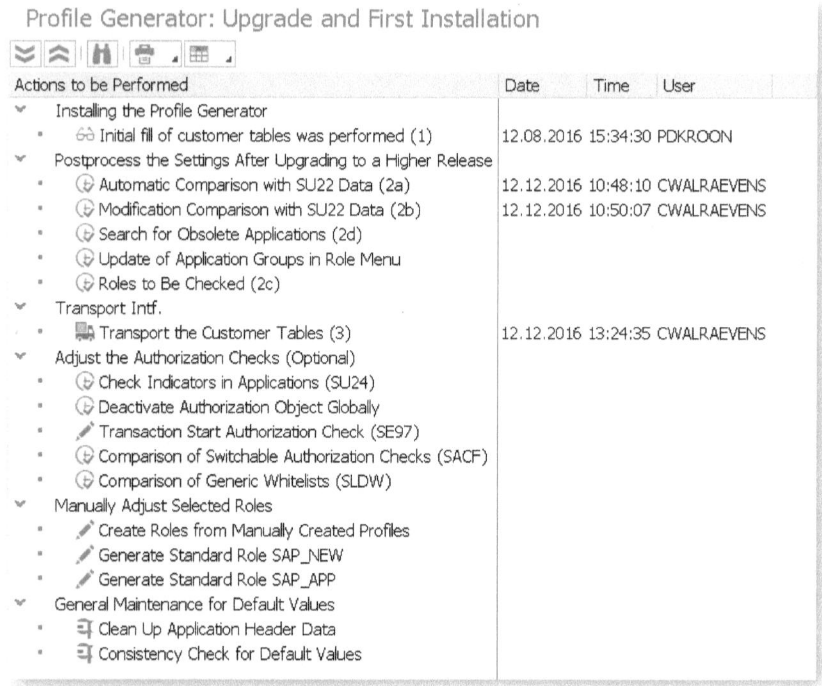
Profile Generator: Upgrade and First Installation

Actions to be Performed	Date	Time	User
Installing the Profile Generator			
Initial fill of customer tables was performed (1)	12.08.2016	15:34:30	PDKROON
Postprocess the Settings After Upgrading to a Higher Release			
Automatic Comparison with SU22 Data (2a)	12.12.2016	10:48:10	CWALRAEVENS
Modification Comparison with SU22 Data (2b)	12.12.2016	10:50:07	CWALRAEVENS
Search for Obsolete Applications (2d)			
Update of Application Groups in Role Menu			
Roles to Be Checked (2c)			
Transport Intf.			
Transport the Customer Tables (3)	12.12.2016	13:24:35	CWALRAEVENS
Adjust the Authorization Checks (Optional)			
Check Indicators in Applications (SU24)			
Deactivate Authorization Object Globally			
Transaction Start Authorization Check (SE97)			
Comparison of Switchable Authorization Checks (SACF)			
Comparison of Generic Whitelists (SLDW)			
Manually Adjust Selected Roles			
Create Roles from Manually Created Profiles			
Generate Standard Role SAP_NEW			
Generate Standard Role SAP_APP			
General Maintenance for Default Values			
Clean Up Application Header Data			
Consistency Check for Default Values			

Figure 1.4: Screen for transaction SU25

Generate derived roles

To keep your derived roles 100% consistent with the single roles they have been derived from, use the GENERATE DERIVED ROLES functionality of PFCG from within your single roles by clicking the icon highlighted in Figure 1.5. This will ensure that the content of the derived roles (except for the organizational values) is kept synchronized with the imparting single role.

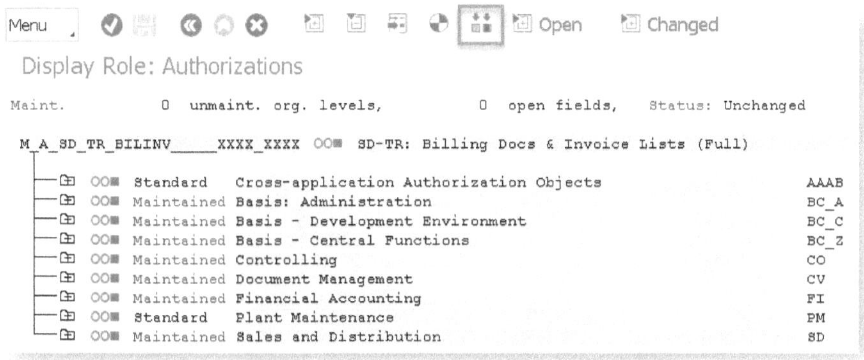

Figure 1.5: The Generate Derived Roles functionality

Organizational levels

The SAP system comes with a standard set of organizational levels. These are authorization object fields with a specific status that allows central maintenance of the field values in PFCG (see Figure 1.6). Indeed, if you have several authorization objects within a role that have that authorization object field, you only have to maintain it once in the role and the central values are propagated to all the objects containing that field. The list of organizational levels is stored in table USORG. The SAP system also comes with standard programs for upgrading authorization object fields to organizational levels. Whenever you need to restrict by a certain field (due to a specific business requirement) and this field is an organizational field, it is strongly recommended that you upgrade this field to an organizational level. For example, PERSONNEL AREA in the HCM module is organizational in nature but is not included in the SAP standard list of organizational levels.

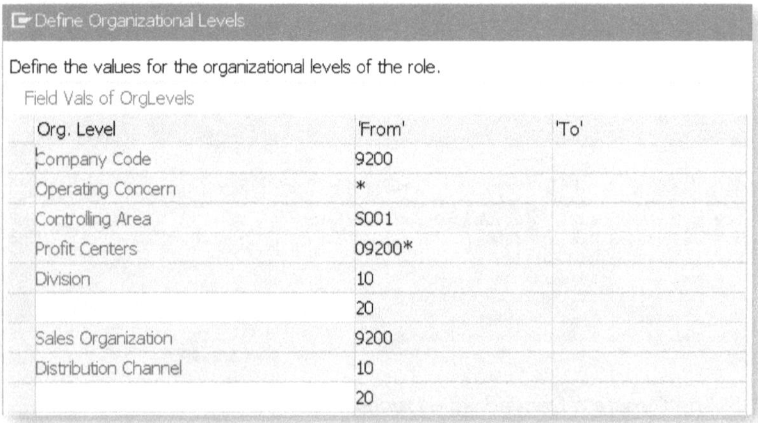

Define Organizational Levels

Define the values for the organizational levels of the role.

Field Vals of OrgLevels

Org. Level	'From'	'To'
Company Code	9200	
Operating Concern	*	
Controlling Area	S001	
Profit Centers	09200*	
Division	10	
	20	
Sales Organization	9200	
Distribution Channel	10	
	20	

Figure 1.6: Example of organizational values in a derived role

Authorization statuses

In PFCG, the authorizations can have one of the following statuses:

- *Standard*: An authorization fully filled with default values from transaction SU24 automatically receives the status *Standard*.
- *Maintained*: An authorization partially filled from transaction SU24 automatically receives the status *Maintained* if the empty fields are maintained.
- *Changed*: An authorization where the proposed default values are overruled in the Profile Generator receives the status *Changed*.
- *Manual*: An authorization manually added to a role automatically receives the status *Manual*. The object cannot be related to any transaction code in the role; in transaction SU24, the authorization object and transaction codes are not linked to each other.

The consequences of having authorizations with status *Manual* or *Changed* are described below, together with relevant solutions:

- An authorization object that has been included manually will never be maintained automatically if the linked transaction code is removed or changed. Therefore, these authorizations must be limited to an absolute minimum.

- A *Changed* authorization means that the default values of the authorization object were overwritten. This implies that the link with the information from transaction SU24 is broken. This may result in a new authorization being imported in the role from the transaction SU24 tables when the role is maintained, leading to a misunderstanding about which information is correct. Therefore, changed authorizations should also be kept to an absolute minimum.

1.1.6 Testing single, derived, and composite roles

The testing approach is important in any authorizations project. Ideally, there should be no business disruption caused by insufficient authorizations during the go-live. Therefore, an appropriate testing approach is required.

Typically, application experts and key users should be involved during the unit testing phase of the single roles to ensure the new single roles work independently of each other. It is crucial that every single role works by itself. There are two important reasons for this:

- When a single role is added to end users in operational mode (after go-live), you have to be certain that the functionality added will work in all cases.
- When a single role has to be removed from an end user, you have to be certain that the remaining authorized functionality remains intact.

This second aspect in particular is fundamental. Too many companies have been paralyzed during position changes and remediation activities, not daring to take away certain access because they were afraid to touch functionality that had to remain authorized. To remain compliant with audit requirements, such as the need-to-have criterion, and to be able to engage in SoD remediation activities, the flexible removal of single roles must be facilitated by the authorizations concept implemented. Testing the single roles thoroughly definitely contributes to meeting this requirement.

You might be wondering whether you should test every derived role as well. In large multinationals with many derived roles, this might involve an enormous effort. Fortunately, it is not necessary to have every derived role tested separately. In fact, if you set up the derived roles correctly, all derived roles are fully consistent with the single role they were derived from. This means that all the non-organizational authorization object fields of the derived roles are identical to the single role they were derived from. The derived roles only differ from their parent in terms of the organizational fields. When those organizational fields are fully documented in an authorization restriction grid document, we can reduce the derived role testing to a full input check which compares the content of the derived roles with the authorization restriction grid document. If you need absolute certainty, you could opt to test a selected derived role domain (instead of testing the parent single role) and perform an input check for the other domains.

End users could be involved during the acceptance testing phase of composite roles to ensure the new composite roles cover their daily job activities. In particular, when a business decides to remove access (e.g., because of SoD violations), the business must check whether the daily processes still work properly. However, we consider this composite role testing as optional. In a pilot user go-live approach (see Section 1.1.7), you could skip the composite role testing and replace it with this pilot user approach.

1.1.7 Going live with new roles

To ensure a smooth go-live, a phased approach is advisable wherever and whenever possible. Ideally, the whole user population to be migrated to the new authorizations setup should be divided into several rollouts. Although it is important to split the go-lives, the recommendation is still to migrate all assigned roles of a user. In other words, the split into rollouts should be done based on regions, countries, sites, etc., allowing complete users to be migrated. A split per business process or SAP module is usually not recommended because such approaches usually mean that not all of a user's authorization roles can be immediately migrated to the new authorizations, resulting in a user being affected multiple times during go-live.

Once the different rollouts have been identified, pilot users for each composite role can be used to reduce the impact of the go-live even further. The principle here is that a limited number of pilot users are transferred to the new authorization roles. Only when no issues occur for these pilot users will their colleagues be transferred in a second phase. If issues occur during the pilot user phase, they are resolved immediately, while colleagues with the old roles ensure business continuity. Any issue will thus occur only once. In the case of complex issues, a rollback to the old authorizations can be considered on a temporary basis.

A big bang approach is required only when no other option is possible. In this type of approach, all users are migrated to the new authorization setup simultaneously on a certain go-live date. Typical examples of this scenario are a greenfield SAP implementation and a new site rollout within an existing SAP system. Needless to say, a big bang approach increases the importance of the test phase and requires much more post-go-live support.

1.1.8 Establishing your governance model

After having performed the implementation steps discussed correctly, you are still not quite there yet. The project has to become a process! For security projects in particular, you must ensure that the—hopefully—correctly implemented setup remains intact during the operational phase. Indeed, new users will enter your systems, leavers will need to lose their access, people will change positions within your company, new functionality and new entities will roll into your SAP processes, audit and SoD requirements might require clean-up and remediation activities, etc. In short, you need a whole set of procedures to enable all these changes, while keeping the authorizations setup in perfect shape.

Whatever maturity level your company is at, you will need at least the following procedures in some form:

- **User administration**: This procedure should describe the way new user IDs are requested and created, how additional access is requested, approved, and provided, how access removals are requested, approved, and executed, how passwords are (re)set, and how user IDs are terminated.
- **Role administration**: Similarly, this procedure should describe how new roles are requested, approved, and created (and accor-

ding to what criteria), how change requests for roles are requested, approved, and administered, and how obsolete roles are decommissioned.

- **Error reporting**: End users must be able to report errors and missing access. This procedure should describe how errors are reported, what the process is for evaluating the validity of these kinds of requests (not all reported errors are valid!), and what the process is for implementing the solution and communicating the solution to the end users.
- **Monitoring**: Finally, all these procedures and the access rights themselves must be monitored. Procedures for dormant user IDs, unused roles, revalidation of assigned roles, risk violations (SoD analysis), etc. must be defined and executed.

To maximize the level of efficiency and control, user and role management processes must be realistic from a business perspective. The involvement of the business is a key success factor for an authorizations project and process. It is essential that business process owners and data owners remain involved in user access and role management processes—to control user access and to keep such access in line with business requirements yet limit risk exposure. These owners are accountable for the risk exposure they allow in their processes when granting users access to their processes and data. Hence, they must be involved and have power of decision over who can access what data. The authorizations concept implemented must allow them to take informed decisions.

Prerequisites for this business owner involvement are:

- The role setup reflects the organization and business (sub)processes
- The role content matches the role description and uses business terminology
- There is a role owner for each role
- Role owners are consulted when role content is changed
- Role owners are consulted when users request access
- The access request informs the role owner of possible risks involved in granting the access

- The effort for business is restricted to a minimum by automation, information availability, management by exception, etc.
- All decisions are documented
- Clear communication in business language

While all of the above are crucial for successful access management, performing all these procedures manually can be a huge task. SAP provides state-of-the-art solutions to support and largely automate these processes: SAP Access Control and SAP Identity Management. Amongst others, these applications provide the following features:

- Automated user creation, (de)provisioning, and termination
- Workflow-driven approval processes for role assignment and role content changes
- Detailed access risk monitoring functionality, including mitigating control documentation
- Embedded risk analysis within the approval flow
- Automated periodic user access and risk reviews
- Extensive use of HCM and/or *Lightweight Directory Access Protocol (LDAP)* as a source to trigger user and role administration processes

1.2 ECC authorizations versus S/4HANA authorizations

As already stated, the authorization mechanisms in S/4HANA remain largely intact and as they were in the SAP ECC releases. This is especially true when Fiori is used only for a small number of specific apps. However, if full-blown Fiori is chosen as the only front end for accessing and using S/4HANA, there is a slight change to the traditional PFCG approach.

What is new to the full Fiori approach is that the Fiori apps, transaction codes, and WebDynpro applications are selected on the front-end server (the SAP NetWeaver Gateway server). Although they are still necessary to grant data access to the back end, the required back-end roles and authorizations are not generated automatically.

In Chapter 2, we will discuss how to set up roles and security on the front-end gateway server for Fiori apps. For now, assume that these steps have already been performed and that only the back-end roles still need to be created. This new aspect is described in this section.

Adding transaction codes and WebDynpro applications to a role menu is something that is very common in role creation. What is new in S/4HANA is the option to also add Fiori *tile catalogs* to a role. You can even do that remotely from the back-end role, connecting to the SAP NetWeaver Gateway system. To do this, perform the following steps:

- In the role menu of PFCG, use the dropdown option (defaulted to *Transaction*) to select SAP FIORI TILE CATALOG (see Figure 1.7).

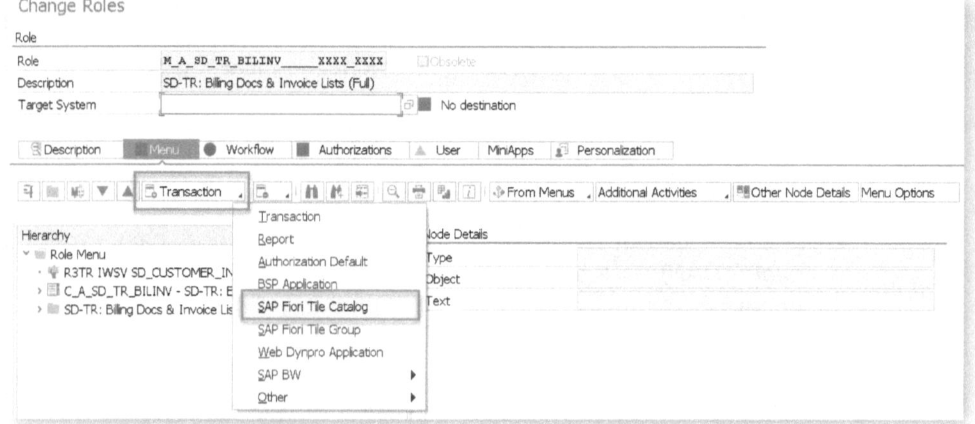

Figure 1.7: Selecting a Fiori tile catalog in a back-end role

- In the dialog box that appears, select REMOTE FRONT-END SERVER. In the RFC DESTINATION field, select your Fiori SAP NetWeaver Gateway system and then choose the catalog ID you would like to import into the role (see Figure 1.8).

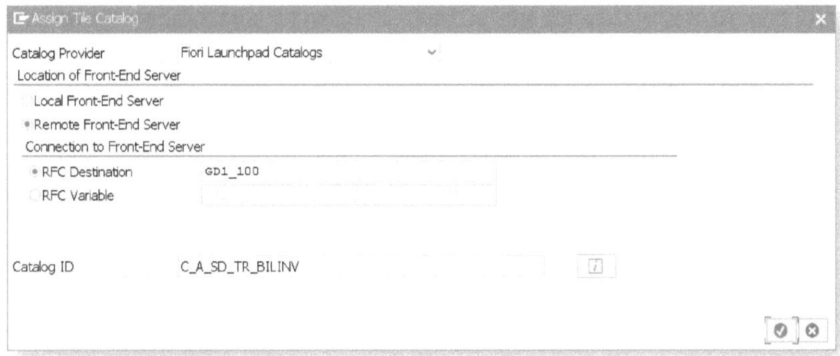

Figure 1.8: Selecting a remote Fiori tile catalog

- Depending on how the selected Fiori tile catalog is built (i.e., the combination of transaction tiles, WebDynpro tiles, and true UI5 Fiori apps), the services and transaction codes required are added to the role menu. In the example below, you can see the combination of a catalog and transaction codes selected directly in a role menu (see Figure 1.9).

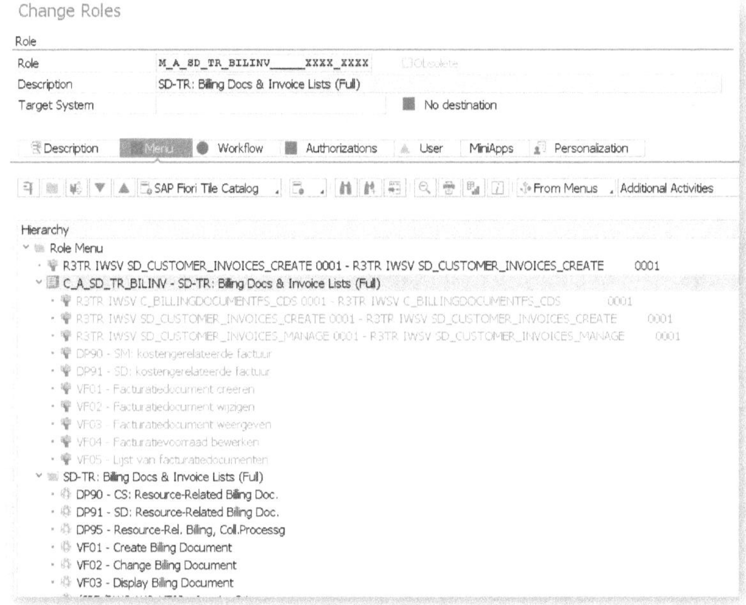

Figure 1.9: The role menu

- The AUTHORIZATIONS tab in PFCG still reacts as before. Based on the content of the role menu and what has been defined in transaction SU24, the AUTHORIZATIONS tab is filled with objects and default values that you need for subsequent maintenance in the same way as before (see Figure 1.10). Note in particular the combination of S_TCODE and S_SERVICE authorizations. Refer to Chapter 2 for more details on this.

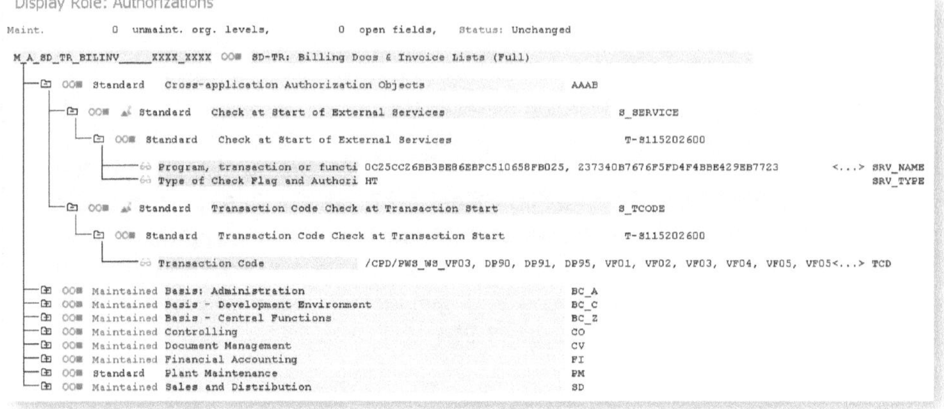

Figure 1.10: The role content

1.3 Conceptual options for SAP roles

During each of the steps described in the previous section, you have to make choices. The difficulty is that none of these choices are necessarily wrong in themselves, especially not when you consider specific company settings, system maturity levels, or project statuses. However, in the long run, when you add up all the choices made, it is always the case that only a very select set of combined choices results in an authorizations concept that is robust in its entirety. Every choice you make when creating roles always has to consider the big picture and has to be made with the highest (future) maturity level in mind. Regardless of whether that top maturity level seems unreachable or even not desirable when you start creating roles, you still need to take the right decisions at each step simply to keep your options open for reaching these higher levels of maturity. In fact, taking wrong decisions at an early stage in the conceptual process will simply block you from going to a next level of maturity at some point in the future. Many companies have seen themselves forced to go through major redesign exercises simply to rectify wrong decisions from the past and to enable them to get to a higher level of security and more mature governance models (including more advanced monitoring procedures, automated provisioning systems, and extensive compliance regulations). In an analogy with real life, you could compare all the decisions to be taken with:

- Building a house: you could start on your own, with great spirit and enthusiasm, designing your own house and building it without the help of experienced craftsmen. You will often start by making some decisions that seem appropriate at one point, only to discover that you get stuck at some later point because you did not anticipate certain aspects. Revising some work is often inevitable in those cases. Considering all these potential future aspects multiple times, like true craftsmen do, certainly helps you to make the right decisions at each phase of a project.
- Solving a labyrinth puzzle: while numerous entry points might present themselves at the beginning of the puzzle, only one set of correct decisions (going left, right, or continuing straight ahead) will get you out of the labyrinth.

Let us take a look at the conceptual options available when using the possible building blocks SAP provides for granting authorizations: single roles, derived roles, and composite roles. We will provide an overview of the options and we will also highlight what we believe to be the advisable option and why.

1.3.1 Single roles

Single roles contain the transaction codes that have to be authorized together with the required authorizations to execute these transaction codes.

Conceptually, the transaction codes can be grouped in two ways:

- **Job-based**: all transaction codes needed to perform a job are grouped into a single role.

- **Process-based**: transaction codes are grouped to authorize specific parts of business processes.

It is our belief that single roles are best designed to grant access to a specific subprocess (see Figure 1.11). In this approach, each single role works independently of the others, giving access only to the described functionality. Because of their granularity, single roles are designed in compliance with SoD rules. Indeed, the subprocess level is also the level at which risk rulesets are defined by auditors. Consequently, having (single) roles and (risk) rules fully aligned will provide the strong foundation required for your authorizations concept.

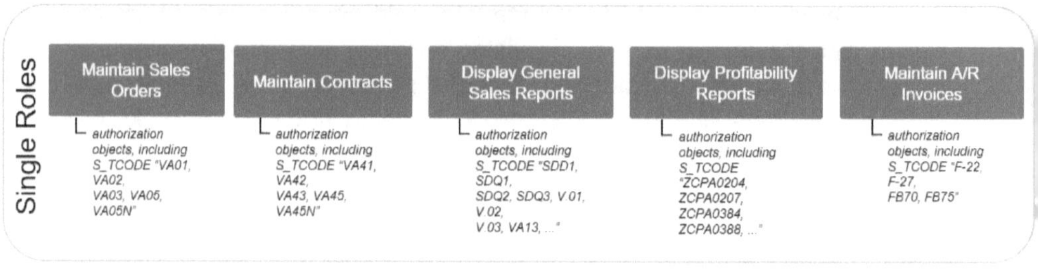

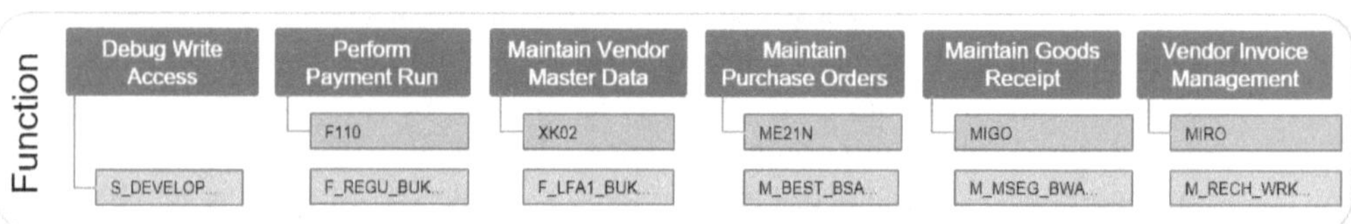

Figure 1.11: Single role design

Let's have a look at the grouping criteria you have to comply with when applying a process-based single role design:

The internal control criterion

Single roles have to be established on the level of a subprocess within the business processes implemented (purchase to pay, order to cash, etc.). This is typically the level at which SoD rules are defined by auditors. Single and derived roles (the lowest technical level in the authorizations concept) must be free of any SoD conflicts.

The homogeneity criterion

Only (very) similar functionality can be combined within the same single role. Transaction codes belonging to different modules (BC, FI, CO, HR, etc.) or even different sub-modules (A/P, A/R, G/L, etc.) must never be combined in one single role. The main goal of this form of grouping is transparency, making the single roles understandable for business people and allowing enhanced ownership. Maintainability is also enhanced with this grouping method: because the number of authorization objects within homogeneous single roles is relatively low, the link between these authorization objects and the transaction codes they protect is much clearer. While there is, of course, some similarity between the homogeneity criterion and the internal control criterion, homogeneity focuses more on transparency and maintainability (more operational considerations). The internal control criterion focuses more on the risk-based monitoring and on ease of remediating potential SoD issues.

The consistency criterion

Custom-developed code and transaction codes have to be incorporated in the single roles in line with the same logic as standard functionality: grouped by process, subprocess, functionality, authorization checks. If some key authorization checks appear to be missing or are insufficient to comply with access restriction requirements, the development team must be instructed about which authorization checks to include in the custom code to bring the functionality developed in-house in line with the standard `AUTHORITY-CHECK` command.

The business process criterion

The authorizations for data and processes must be defined in line with the execution of the business processes. Authorizations and roles do not exist for their own benefit; they exist only to grant access to and to protect business processes and business data. If business subprocesses are spread over different people (the well-known process swim lanes), the role concept implemented has to facilitate the assignment of authorizations to the specified steps of the process. It should also be possible to limit access to confidential data. However, complexity should be managed to ensure long-term sustainability—the only reason for restricting access even further would be a potential risk.

The ownership criterion

The business owners must be able to rely on the role descriptions to understand the access a certain role is granting to users. For example, if a role is described as giving access to maintain sales orders, it should do exactly that: give users the right to create, change, and display sales orders, nothing more, nothing less. Adequate role ownership can be established only when this consistency is achieved.

A strong naming convention

A crucial aspect in establishing all of the above is having a strong and clear role-naming convention. The following indicators should be present in any naming convention for single roles:

- A landscape indicator (e.g.: S4)
- A role type indicator (e.g.: S for single role)
- An access type indicator (e.g.: A for all; V for view)
- A module/sub-module indicator (e.g.: MMPU)
- A subprocess indicator (e.g.: PURORD)

Example of a single role name:

- Technical name: S4_S_A_MMPU_PURORD
- Description: Purchase Orders (All)

1.3.2 Derived roles

As discussed in Section 1.1.2, organizational restrictions (company codes, plants, sales organizations, etc.) can be translated into derived roles. Although this is optional (you could implement organizational restrictions in separate single roles), we strongly recommend using derived roles for transparency and consistency. Derived roles inherit the transaction codes (the menu) from the single role they refer to, enforcing strong consistency between these roles. Derived roles are useful when different organizational restrictions are used for the same set of transaction codes (functionality). The inheritance from the imparting role relates to the transaction codes and all non-organizational level fields in the imparting role. Only the organizational levels have to be maintained separately for each derived role.

It is strongly recommended that you maintain SAP authorization roles in compliance with SAP standard functionality. Here again, taking the correct design decisions will allow you to use the SAP standard functionality optimally and to lower your role maintenance efforts.

The following best practices apply:

- Maintain functional restrictions (authorization object field values that are not defined as an organizational level) at single role level and propagate these towards the derived roles.
- Maintain organizational level restrictions at derived role level.
- Upgrade non-organizational fields in the SAP back-end systems to organizational levels when needed and where possible. The SAP system comes with standard programs for doing this.
- Maintain transaction SU24 data: all authorizations included in a role should be linked to the correct transaction code in the USOBT(X)_C tables to ensure role quality and to facilitate future maintenance.
- Deactivate all authorizations not needed in a single and derived role to avoid *access creep*, accumulation of access rights, and unexpected SoD conflicts.

Furthermore, a strong naming convention should be applied. The following indicators should be present in any naming convention for derived roles:

- A landscape indictor (e.g.: S4)
- A role type indicator (e.g.: D for derived role)
- An access type indicator (e.g.: A for all; V for view)
- A module/sub-module indicator (e.g.: MMPU)

- A subprocess indicator (e.g.: PURORD)
- An organizational restriction indicator (e.g.: 1000)

Example of a derived role name:

- Technical name: S4_D_A_MMPU_PURORD_1000
- Description: Purchase Orders (All)—CC 1000

These principles ensure consistency and efficiency in role maintenance activities. Furthermore, to ensure that user access can be approved by role owners (business people), and to enable automated user provisioning, it is essential that the role descriptions are formulated in clear business language and correspond with the actual access granted by the role.

1.3.3 Composite roles

As the term already suggests, *composite roles* contain a set of single and/or derived roles. Conceptually, the following basic options are available:

- **Only direct single and derived role assignments**: Composite roles are optional. It is technically possible to assign single and derived roles directly to users.
- **A hybrid model combining composite role assignments with single and derived role assignments**: Composite roles are especially useful for facilitating the user provisioning and for establishing consistency in granting access rights. Grouping access (single and derived roles) into composite roles makes it easier to assign these blocks of access simultaneously. Certain exceptions and/or SoD-relevant critical access could be omitted from the composite role design and could be assigned separately and directly to users for tighter control reasons.

- **Only composite role assignments**: Using the advantages of composite roles (provisioning, consistency) to their full extent, you could opt to only assign composite roles and to not allow the direct assignment of single and derived roles. In such a setup, the content of a composite role must be in line with the subprocesses (the swim lanes) a user/group of users has/have to execute to perform their daily job. This method of working corresponds to the business role approach (see Figure 1.12).

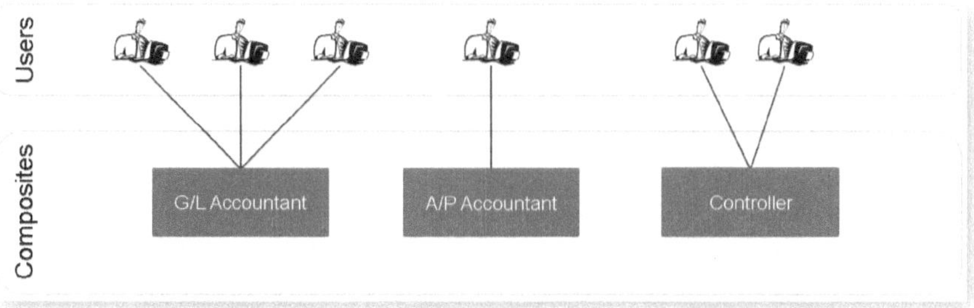

Figure 1.12: Assignments of composite roles to users

We believe that the business role approach (using only composite roles to grant access) is the most advisable one. However, we also believe that not all companies are (already) mature enough to achieve this.

If a company's business processes are not identical in different entities and/or countries, it will be very difficult to apply the pure business role approach. In those cases, the hybrid model will bring a solution to the table. What is essential in a hybrid model is that the exceptions are strictly defined and described. As long as the exceptions remain the exceptions (and do not become the rule), this is a working solution as well.

Finally, for smaller companies, the direct single role and derived role assignment scenario might be sufficient.

1.4 Cross-landscape authorizations concept

In the previous sections, we discussed the different aspects of the logical access security in S/4HANA. In the next two chapters, we will highlight the specifics for the Fiori and HANA database security. Although it is essential to master the security techniques of each of these three systems, this will still not bring you home.

These three systems do not work independently of one another:

- When you present Fiori tiles to the end user via PFCG tile roles (see Chapter 2 for the details), each visible tile has to work properly. To achieve this, you need not only the correct front-end authorizations on the gateway system but also adequate back-end authorizations to make the tile work. Depending on the tile itself, the back-end system can be very different: for the tiles that are more like traditional transaction code, you will need adequate S/4HANA authorizations; for native UI5 applications using the HANA database directly, you will need adequate HANA privileges and roles (see Chapter 3 for the details).
- You also have to ensure that all tiles are available to the end user according to what the end user is authorized to do on the back end. In contrast to what we are used to, we are no longer presenting the whole SAP menu to the end user. The aim of Fiori is to present a highly customized and personalized user interface to the end user. This interface must be fully in line with what the end user is allowed to do on the different back-end systems.
- Regardless of whether the end user is executing functionality through the S/4HANA application (secured via the S/4HANA application authorizations) or whether the end user is accessing the HANA database directly via native applications, the dataset is the same. Consequently, the criteria for securing this data should be identical. The fact that the security mechanisms are significantly different at the technical level does not change that requirement.

> On the contrary, it is the duty of the security architect to design the security model conceptually in such a way that the different mechanisms result in a coherent and consistent concept. This model must ensure that your business data is protected in exactly the same way (applying the same set of criteria) regardless of the way the end user is accessing the data: through the S/4HANA application, through native HANA applications, through BW/4HANA, etc.

So, on the one hand, we know that the security mechanisms are different depending on the system (see this and the following chapters for the details), and on the other hand, we know we have to apply the same security rules consistently across the landscape because we consume the same data through different applications. To achieve this, we believe the following aspects are crucial to a successful security model:

- You have to translate the technical specifics of each system into one homogeneous security model. If you opt for a business role approach (discussed earlier in this chapter), you have to translate the technical layer of each system into that business role concept: on the Fiori side, you have to design your catalogs, groups, and tile roles in such a way that fits with that business role approach; on the S/4HANA application, you have to design the single roles, the derived roles, and the composite roles in such a way that fits with your business role concept; on the HANA database, you have to design your views, native applications, privileges, and roles in such a way that fits with the business role setup. Although this goes beyond the scope of this book, this approach also applies to all other systems in your landscape (BW/4HANA, SuccessFactors, Hybris, CRM, SRM, etc.) as well.
- Once you have translated the specific mechanisms on each system into the same conceptual approach, you have to link the different concepts across the systems. We strongly believe that you have to do this through naming conventions.

Figure 1.13 summarizes our approach to achieving a consistent cross-system authorizations concept in an S/4HANA environment:

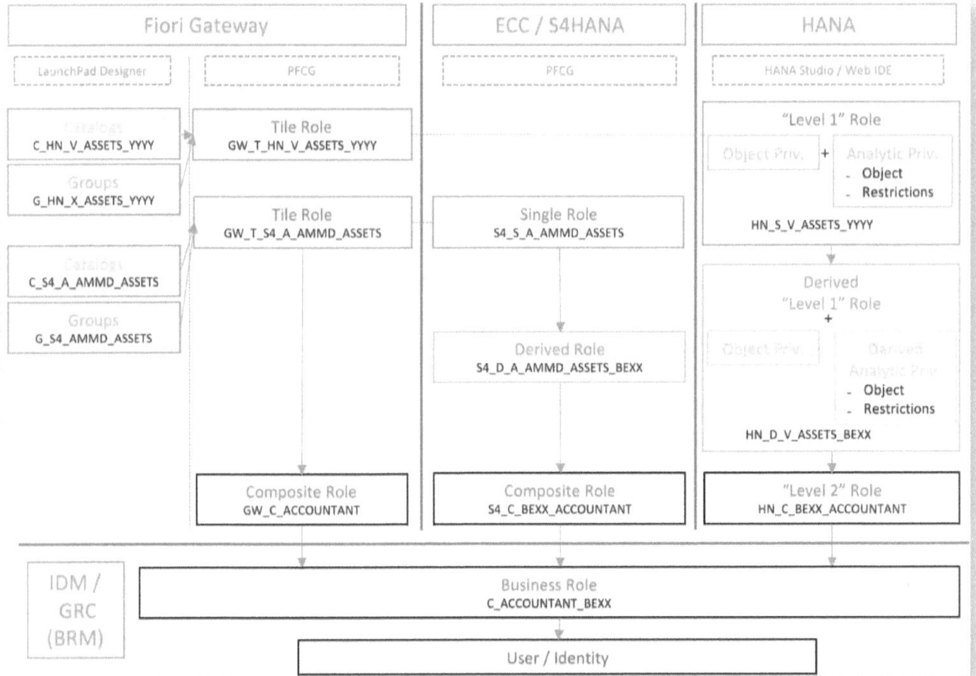

Figure 1.13: Cross-landscape authorizations concept

The key to the naming convention is that there is a clear link between the names of the different objects across the systems:

- For Fiori tiles using S/4HANA functionality, there must be a clear naming link between the Fiori catalogs, the Fiori groups, the tile roles on the gateway system, and the back-end single roles granting access to the particular functionality. In the example in Figure 1.13, this link is established by indicating that the catalog, the group, the tile role, and the back-end role all refer to granting access to asset master data (A_AMMD_ASSETS).

- For Fiori tiles accessing the data directly on the HANA database, there must be a clear naming link between the Fiori catalogs, the Fiori groups, the tile roles on the gateway system, and the HANA (single) roles granting access to particular apps, views, and/or data. In the example in Figure 1.13, this link is established by indicating that the catalog, the group, the tile role, and the HANA role all refer to granting display access to asset master data (V_ASSETS).
- The naming of the tile roles must also point to the back-end system the tile roles are created for. We do not combine tiles pointing to different back-end systems into one tile role. For transparency reasons, we recommend that you create separate tile roles for different back-end systems.
- The scope of this book is S4/HANA, including Fiori and HANA security. In a real-life case, the SAP system landscape will be even more complex, including BW, SuccessFactors, CRM, Hybris, SRM, etc. We are convinced that in the future, Fiori will also be used as the front end for these systems as well. This will only increase the need for a consistent cross-system security concept to keep the security transparent and sustainable.

Once the naming convention links are established between the catalogs, groups, tile roles, single roles on S/4HANA, and level 1 roles on HANA, these objects can be (optionally) grouped into composite roles (on the gateway and on S/4HANA) and into level 2 roles on HANA. This approach can then be further extended into a business role concept using professional applications such as SAP Access Control and/or SAP Identity Management. Using this type of concept allows you to easily determine and even automatically provide the necessary access a user needs in all the different systems within an IT landscape based on the user's job within the company.

2 Securing Fiori

SAP Fiori is a new user experience (UX) for SAP software and applications. It provides a set of applications that are used in regular business functions such as work approvals, financial apps, calculation apps, and various self-service apps.

The SAP user interface, or SAP GUI as we know it today, was first introduced in 1992 together with the official release of SAP R/3. SAP R/3, the client server edition, was the successor to the SAP R/2 release, the mainframe edition. Although SAP has made several attempts to modernize SAP GUI, an end user from the time it was introduced would still find their way around today. Many transactions and screens have remained the same or changed very little. Since the initial release of SAP GUI, SAP has released several alternative user interfaces such as the SAP Workplace (which was part of the mySAP.com offering), the SAP Enterprise Portal, and the NetWeaver Business Client or NWBC. None were as successful as SAP GUI except, perhaps, for the NetWeaver Business Client. The NetWeaver Business Client is, however, an extension to the SAP GUI. The conclusion of all this is that although many people complained about the old-fashioned look of SAP GUI, they kept using it and will probably continue to do so in the future.

But there is no denying the fact that the user community is changing fast. The SAP users of tomorrow are the youngsters of today, who are used to accessing data from their mobile devices. To them, SAP GUI is a relic from the dark ages. This shift is not limited to youngsters—many end users want data access from any device, from any place, at any time. SAP released SAP Fiori to respond to this demand. SAP Fiori is built using modern design principles you might expect from applications designed for smartphones and tablets. There are already more than 500 role-based Fiori applications such as for HR, Finance, and Business Intelligence. An SAP Fiori application is always limited to a specific task or activity. The design is responsive and deployable on multiple platforms.

There are three types of SAP Fiori applications: transactional apps, fact sheets, and analytical apps.

- **Transactional or task-based applications**: The transactional SAP Fiori applications are limited to specific tasks such as entering a holiday request or expense note. They give end users fast access to data and represent a simplified view of an existing business process or workflow.
- **Fact sheets**: Fact sheets have far more capabilities than transactional applications. From a fact sheet, you can drill down into the details. You can even navigate from one fact sheet to another or jump to the related transactional applications. For fact sheets, the underlying database must be SAP HANA. An example of a fact sheet is an application that shows the overview and details of a piece of equipment and its maintenance schedule.
- **Analytical applications**: Analytical applications build on business intelligence using the capabilities of SAP HANA. They allow you to monitor key performance indicators (KPIs) of your business operations and to react immediately as changes occur. An example is the sales orders application, which immediately shows your sales representative the sales history from his customer, allowing him to take discount decisions immediately.

2.1 Deployment options

SAP Fiori apps consist of front-end components, which provide the user interface and the connection to the back end, and back-end components, which provide the data. The front-end components and the back-end components are delivered in separate products and must be installed in a system landscape that is enabled for SAP Fiori. There are multiple deployment options for the SAP Fiori components, each with their respective advantages and disadvantages. SAP Fiori applications are accessed through the SAP NetWeaver Gateway. The gateway consists of two components: *SAP Gateway Foundation (SAP_GWFND)* and *User Interface Technology (SAP_UI)*. Both components are add-ons, which from NetWeaver version 7.4, are part of the SAP NetWeaver ABAP Stack. With NetWeaver 7.31, the components had to be deployed separately. This means that any system built on SAP NetWeaver, such as SAP ERP or SAP CRM, can be used to deploy SAP Fiori applications.

The following deployment options exist: *central hub deployment*, the *embedded scenario* and the *cloud edition* (see Figure 2.1).

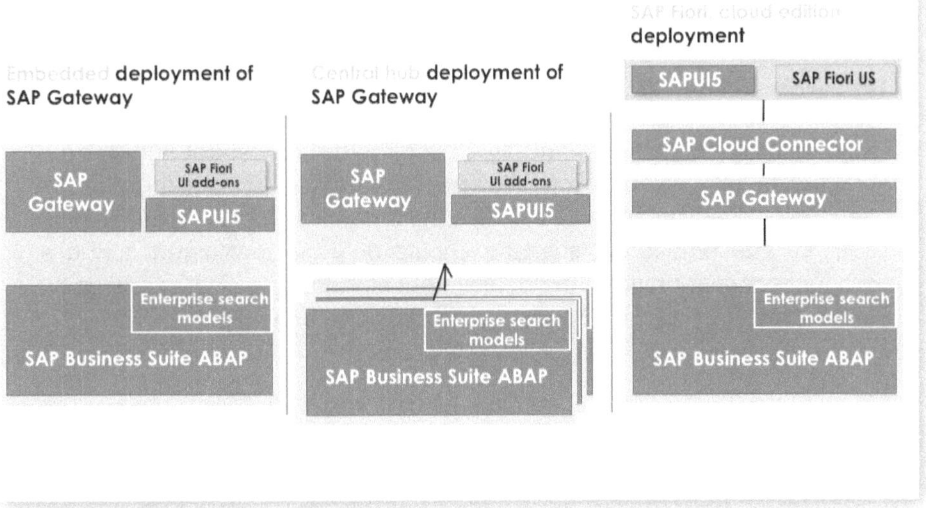

Figure 2.1: SAP Fiori deployment options

2.1.1 Central hub deployment

The central hub deployment is the preferred option. Here, SAP NetWeaver Gateway is installed as a separate system. The Fiori applications are deployed here and access the data on the back-end business systems, such as SAP ERP or SAP CRM. Although this option implies an extra system, thus a higher total cost of ownership (TCO), it enables a multi-back-end system scenario while ensuring a consistent look and feel for the different applications. The central hub can be considered a single point of access for all mobile applications. In addition, installing SAP NetWeaver Gateway on a separate system allows you to move the system behind or in front of the firewall depending on your current network topology and security requirements.

2.1.2 Embedded scenario

SAP NetWeaver is the basis of all ABAP-based SAP applications, regardless of whether you are talking about SAP ERP, SAP BW, or any of the others. As the gateway is an add-on for SAP NetWeaver, it is available on every ABAP-based business application. This means that it can be activated and that Fiori applications can be deployed on any system. This makes an extra system unnecessary. However, we do not recommend the embedded scenario as, in contrast to the central hub deployment, it results in Fiori applications being installed all over the place—negating the advantage of the single point of access for all mobile applications. The embedded scenario should only be considered during a proof of concept or when the deployment of mobile applications is going to be limited to a single SAP application such as SAP ERP.

2.1.3 Cloud edition

The SAP Fiori cloud edition is a ready-to-use infrastructure which can serve as a front end while leaving the back-end systems on premise. The connection to the SAP Fiori Cloud is realized via *SAP Cloud Connector*, which must be installed on premise. The back-end components still have to be installed on the back-end systems.

2.1.4 Comparison of the deployment options

Table 2.1 compares the different deployment options. Every deployment option has its respective advantages and disadvantages. The importance of the pros and cons differ in every customer situation.

We strongly recommend the central hub deployment option as it enables a single point of access to your mobile applications for SAP ERP, SAP BW, and many others, while at the same time ensuring the same look and feel. Due to its limitations and dependencies, the embedded scenario should only be considered in a proof-of-concept scenario.

	Central hub deployment	Embedded deployment	Cloud edition
Access	Enables single point of access to multi-back-end scenarios while ensuring a consistent look and feel across back ends	No single point of access for mobile applications	Enables single point of access to multi-back-end scenarios while ensuring a consistent look and feel across back ends
Dependencies	Update dependencies of front-end and back-end components must be considered	One system, dependencies will occur	Update dependencies of front-end and back-end components must be considered
Landscape	Extra SAP landscape and thus a higher TCO	No additional system required	No additional system required
Network	SAP Gateway can be installed in the demilitarized zone (DMZ)	Complicates network topology and security, as many systems may need to be accessible from the outside	SAP Cloud Connector can be installed in the demilitarized zone (DMZ)

Table 2.1: Comparison of the deployment options

2.2 SAP landscape

As stated above, we strongly recommend the central hub deployment option as it allows a single point of access to all mobile applications. As such, the final SAP landscape will contain the following components: the mobile device, an SAP Web Dispatcher or reverse proxy, the ABAP gateway or front-end server, and one or more back-end systems (see Figure 2.2).

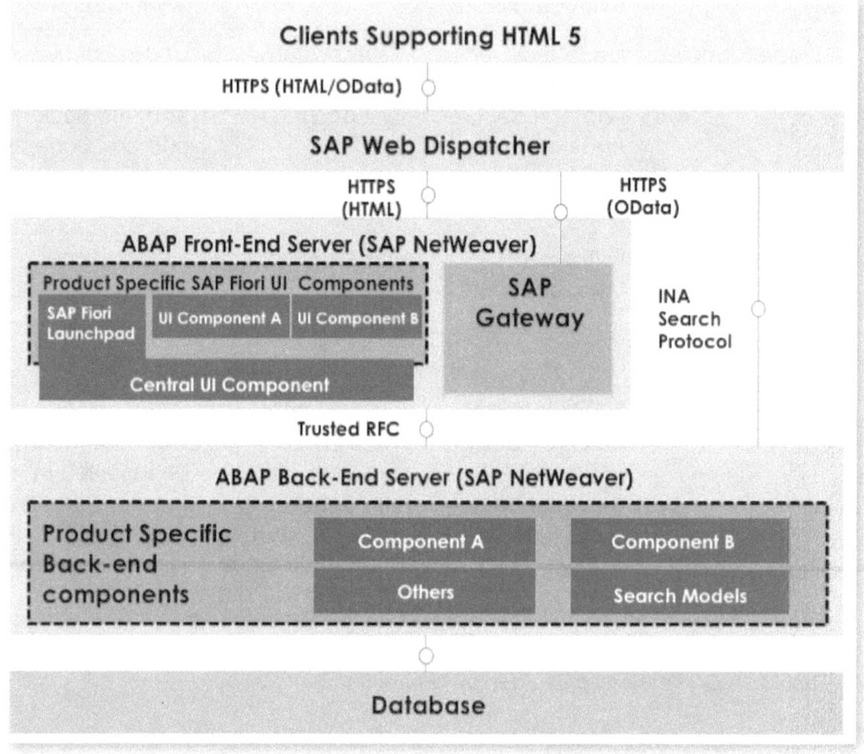

Figure 2.2: The components in the SAP landscape

2.2.1 The mobile device or client

SAP Fiori applications can be accessed from within an Internet browser or from mobile devices running iOS, Android, and Windows. With an Internet browser, you need HTML5 support to run the SAP Fiori applications. For mobile devices running iOS or Android, an SAP Fiori Mobile Client app is available which can be downloaded from iTunes or Google Play.

2.2.2 SAP Web Dispatcher

SAP Web Dispatcher is a software firewall or reverse proxy. It is the single point of entry for all HTTPS requests to the SAP systems. It can accept or reject connections and supports SSL and URL filtering and redirecting. When a connection is accepted, SAP Web Dispatcher balances the load between the different application servers to ensure load balancing. SAP Web Dispatcher can be used as an access point to NetWeaver ABAP and Java systems.

2.2.3 The central hub or front-end server

The front-end components are installed on the central hub or front-end server. The User Interface Technology (SAP_UI) component contains the central UI framework which provides the common infrastructure for all SAP Fiori applications. The *SAP Fiori launchpad* is the basis for all Fiori applications and provides fundamental functions such as logon, surface sizing, navigation between applications, and access to the application catalog. SAP Gateway Foundation (SAP_GWFND) takes care of the communication between the client applications and the back-end systems using *OData services* via *trusted RFC*. With trusted RFC, the password is no longer sent from the trusted to the trusting system. This means that the user only has to be authenticated when connecting to the front-end server and not when data is accessed from the back-end server.

2.2.4 ABAP back-end server or business application

On the ABAP back-end server or business application, the Fiori back-end components provide the business logic—including users, roles, authorizations, and data access. The back-end components are delivered as add-on products which must be installed separately.

2.3 Implementing Fiori authentication

The authentication options for SAP Fiori are similar to those available for other SAP front-end solutions such as SAP GUI, SAP NetWeaver Business Client, and SAP Enterprise Portal. The standard authentication option, and probably still the one most widely used, is the combination of user name and password. This is available out of the box and requires no configuration except for setting password restrictions. Many customers use the *Security Assertion Markup Language (SAML)* authentication methodology as it enables users to connect using their *Microsoft Active Directory* accounts or company e-mail address. SAML also reduces the number of user names and passwords and allows you to enforce a company-wide password policy across all applications. Another option is *certificate authentication*. In this option, an X.509 certificate must be installed on the device used to access the SAP Fiori application. Certificates can be installed on both Windows desktops (and laptops) as well as mobile devices (iOS, Windows 10 Mobile, and Android). This option shifts security from the user to the device. Procedures should be in place to deal with device theft, loss, and replacement.

2.3.1 Basic or out-of-the-box authentication

In this scenario, everyone using a given SAP system receives an SAP user ID and password—no more, no less. The user is created in the gateway and the necessary roles are assigned. When the user connects to the SAP Fiori launchpad, the system requests a user ID and password. Authentication is only required on the front-end sever; connection to the back-end systems is achieved through trusted RFC. User authorizations and roles are therefore separated between the front-end and back-end servers.

2.3.2 Kerberos/SPNEGO

Kerberos is an authentication protocol based on tickets or tokens. It allows users and applications to verify each other's identity. *SPNEGO* is a negotiation mechanism. It is used when a user wants to authenticate to a remote application and is unsure of which protocol the other application supports. Both Kerberos and SPNEGO are part of the SAP *Single Sign-On*

(SSO) product. Using Kerberos and SPNEGO, a trust relationship is established between the front-end and the back-end NetWeaver ABAP or Java server. When users log on to their desktop, their user name and password are verified against the Microsoft Active Directory. For any subsequent logon to the SAP applications, a Kerberos token is used. If you access SAP Fiori apps from within your corporate network, you can enable Kerberos/SPNEGO authentication for the SAP Fiori front-end server.

The Kerberos/SPNEGO authentication has the following advantages:

- Users only have to supply a user name and password when connecting from their desktop. A separate logon to the SAP Fiori server is not required.
- It is supported for both SAP GUI and HTTP access, which simplifies the single sign-on setup
- It is also supported on mobile devices

The disadvantage of Kerberos/SPNEGO is that it requires access to the *identity provider*. This system is normally only accessible from within the corporate network. Kerberos/SPNEGO can therefore only be used after the initiation of a *VPN connection*. This means that Kerberos/SPNEGO cannot be used for most *Internet-facing* deployment scenarios.

2.3.3 X.509 certificates

It should not come as a shock that passwords are not that reliable. In spite of the many guidelines and warnings, people still use the first names of loved ones, the name of their dog, or birthdates as passwords. System-enforced password restrictions result in passwords and user names being written on Post-it notes. Digital certificates may be an alternative—using certificate authentication enables business users to authenticate themselves without the need to enter a user ID or password. The user is prompted to select a certificate to use when connecting to the Gateway.

X.509 is a standard that defines the format of public key certificates. X.509 is used in many Internet protocols, including TLS/SSL, which is the basis for HTTPS, the secure protocol for the Internet. An X.509 certificate contains a public and private key. The certificate is either signed by a certified authority or is self-signed. When a certified authority signs the certificate, you can rely on the public key to establish a secure communication with another party, using the private key to sign the certificate.

If you already have a *public key infrastructure (PKI)* in place, you can use it with SAP Fiori. As the PKI does not require a system to log on to, it can be used in Internet-facing scenarios. It is also supported with SAP GUI, which simplifies a single sign-on setup within your system landscape.

X.509 certificates must be distributed to the workstations and devices that are used to access SAP Fiori apps. For mobile devices, this distribution can be performed centrally by mobile device management software, for example *SAP Afaria*. Device security becomes crucial in this scenario, as device access means access to applications and data. Procedures must be in place to revoke certificates—for example, if the device is stolen or lost.

2.3.4 Security Assertion Markup Language 2.0 (SAML 2.0)

Security Assertion Markup Language (SAML) is an open standard for exchanging authentication and authorization data between two parties. The most important use case is single sign-on. SAML 2.0 is the successor to the initial version. It uses security tokens to authenticate and authorize an end user between an *identity provider (IdP)* and a *service provider*. The identity provider is a system that manages identity information for users and provides authentication services to other trusted service providers. In other words, once the identity provider has successfully authenticated a user, this user is allowed to connect to the service provider. A service provider provides a service or an application to the end users; in our scenario, it is the SAP NetWeaver Gateway server or gateway. The gateway must be configured as a service provider and a trusted connection must be set up with the identity provider. The identity provider can be any software solution, such as Microsoft Active Directory, SAP NetWeaver Identity Management, CA Federation Manager, Oracle Identity Federation 11g, or cloud-based SAML-compliant IdPs.

During logon, SAML 2.0 authentication requires access to an issuing system or identity provider. To enable single sign-on with SAML 2.0 in Internet-facing deployment scenarios that leverage its federation capabilities, you must ensure that the SAML identity provider is securely accessible from outside your corporate network.

2.3.5 SAP logon tickets

An *SAP logon ticket* represents user credentials in one or more SAP systems. It can be used as a single sign-on mechanism with SAP GUI and Web browsers and allows users to connect to the SAP system without entering a user name or password. The gateway server can issue SAP logon tickets.

Although the use of SAP logon tickets is straightforward, there are many prerequisites, for example:

- User names must be the same for all SAP systems
- Web browsers must be configured to accept cookies
- As logon tickets are browser cookies, all systems must be located in the same DNS domain

We do not recommend the use of SAP logon tickets due to the above prerequisites and limitations. X.509 certificates and SAML 2.0 provide additional security features and are applicable in more scenarios. We therefore recommend that you use those options instead of SAP logon tickets.

2.3.6 SAP Authenticator

The *SAP Authenticator mobile application* is an application that generates passcodes for systems that require one-time password authentication. The *time-based one-time password (TOTP)* algorithm computes a one-time passcode from a shared secret key and the current time. Passcodes are time-based and are valid for one logon attempt, which means that they are more secure than common static passwords and users do not have to remember them (i.e., do not have to write them down on a Post-it note). SAP Authenticator is available on iOS and Android devices. It requires an SAML 2.0 identity provider. The TOTP software is an add-on module for SAP NetWeaver Application Server for Java and is part of the SAP Single Sign-On 3.0 product.

Users can connect to the SAP Fiori application by starting *SAP Fiori Client* or by clicking the SAP Fiori bookmark from SAP Authenticator (see Figure 2.3). This initiates the authentication process. SAP Authenticator generates a new passcode and sends it, together with the user name, to SAP Fiori Client. SAP Fiori Client opens a connection to the identity provider. Next, the IdP issues a SAML 2.0 assertion for this user and a connection is opened to the service provider, in this case the gateway server.

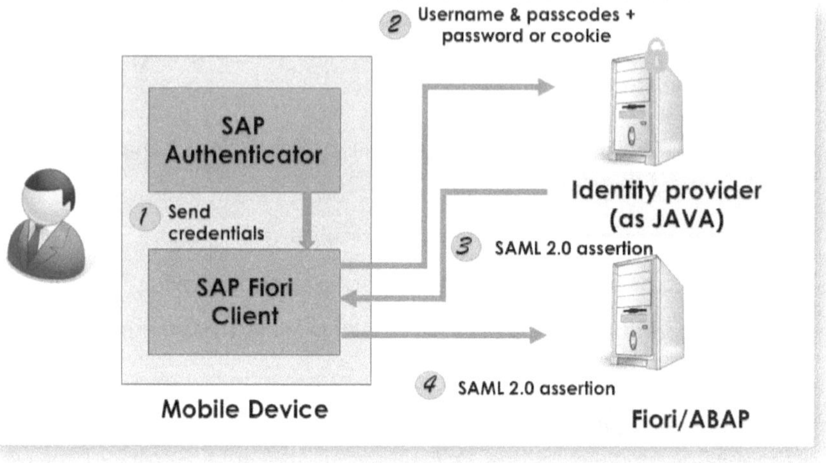

Figure 2.3: The authentication process with SAP Authenticator

To enhance security further, instead of using a single-factor authentication, you can use a two-factor authentication. Single-factor authentication is based on only a single passcode generated and sent by SAP Authenticator. With two-factor authentication, the IdP expects two consecutive passcodes. The second passcode can be based on a persistent cookie issued at the first logon of the user and used to identify the client. This cookie allows the user to use single-factor authentication until the cookie expires or is revoked by the IdP.

Accounts and applications can easily be added to SAP Authenticator, either manually—by creating the account and entering the application URL—or automatically by providing the confirmation code for the account and assigned applications or scanning the QR code for the application.

Both SAP Authenticator and SAP Fiori Client offer password protection. Once a password has been set, access to SAP Fiori Client is possible only after supplying a password. This password is not related to the authentication to the back-end server. It is just a layer of extra application security which can be set as an option.

2.4 Implementing Fiori authorizations

The Fiori launchpad displays available functionality in the form of tiles. Fiori tiles are rectangular objects that provide access to applications. The SAP Fiori *launchpad designer* is a browser-based designer tool for configuring the tiles on the launchpad. In the launchpad designer, logical groups of tiles called catalogs and groups are configured.

The configured tiles are displayed on the Fiori launchpad based on the user's roles. In addition, as is the case within all SAP solutions, the user also needs specific authorizations to be able to use Fiori apps. The SAP role maintenance transaction PFCG is where the configured catalogs and groups are linked to the end user's roles.

We will now discuss the implementation steps for a central hub deployment. These steps are also applicable for the embedded scenario.

2.4.1 Fiori catalogs

Fiori catalogs are logical collections of apps or tiles. Depending on the roles and the catalogs assigned to the roles, the user can browse through the catalogs, choose apps from these catalogs, and add them to the entry page of the SAP Fiori launchpad. Catalogs define the set of all tiles that users can use to personalize the home page.

SAP delivers predefined catalog content for the SAP Fiori launchpad. As an administrator, you can use the launchpad designer to copy and adapt the content in the configuration and customizing scopes. The predefined SAP Fiori launchpad content is stored in the following scopes (see Table 2.2):

Scope	Description	Tool
Configuration	System-wide settings The content delivered by SAP is stored in the configuration scope. Administrators can use the configuration scope to copy a catalog. Then they adapt the copied catalog in the customizing scope for a selected client. To access the launchpad designer in the configuration scope, add parameter scope=CONF to the URL.	SAP Fiori launchpad designer
Customizing	Client-specific settings Content changes are valid only for the current client. These settings supersede configuration settings but can be superseded by personalization settings. Administrators can use the customizing scope to copy a catalog and to adapt it for the selected client. If you access the launchpad designer without providing any scope parameter in the URL, the customizing scope is selected by default. The parameter you can add to the URL is scope=CUST.	SAP Fiori launchpad designer
Personalization	User-specific settings End users can use the personalization scope to adapt a group that contains predefined content and that has been assigned to their user role by an administrator. They can rearrange the tiles in the SAP Fiori launchpad and save their preferences in the personalization layer. These settings supersede customizing and configuration settings.	SAP Fiori launchpad

Table 2.2: Configuration and customizing scopes

To configure the catalog, the user must log in to the launchpad designer and perform the following configuration:

- Create the catalog.
- Add tiles to the catalog: this can be done manually, creating tiles from scratch (e.g., for apps developed in-house), or by referencing to the SAP standard catalogs and tiles. The latter is advisable, as updates to tiles by SAP will also be applied to your custom catalogs when you apply new service packs (see Figure 2.4).

Figure 2.4: Example of the tile part of a catalog

- Add target mappings to the catalog: as with tiles, target mappings can be added manually to your custom catalog or by referencing to SAP standard catalogs (see Figure 2.5).

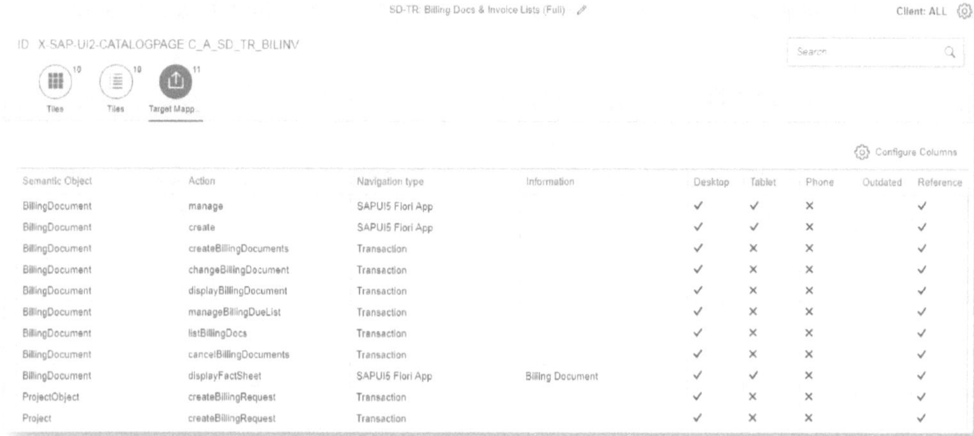

Semantic Object	Action	Navigation type	Information	Desktop	Tablet	Phone	Outdated	Reference
BillingDocument	manage	SAPUI5 Fiori App		✓	✓	×		✓
BillingDocument	create	SAPUI5 Fiori App		✓	✓	×		✓
BillingDocument	createBillingDocuments	Transaction		✓	×	×		✓
BillingDocument	changeBillingDocument	Transaction		✓	×	×		✓
BillingDocument	displayBillingDocument	Transaction		✓	×	×		✓
BillingDocument	manageBillingDueList	Transaction		✓	×	×		✓
BillingDocument	listBillingDocs	Transaction		✓	×	×		✓
BillingDocument	cancelBillingDocuments	Transaction		✓	×	×		✓
BillingDocument	displayFactSheet	SAPUI5 Fiori App	Billing Document	✓	✓	×		✓
ProjectObject	createBillingRequest	Transaction		✓	×	×		✓
Project	createBillingRequest	Transaction		✓	×	×		✓

Figure 2.5: Example of the target mapping part of a catalog

2.4.2 Fiori groups

Fiori groups are subsets of catalogs that contain the apps visible on the SAP Fiori launchpad entry page. The tiles displayed by default on a user's entry page depend on the groups assigned to the user's roles. In addition, the user can personalize the entry page by adding or removing apps to pre-delivered groups or self-defined groups. However, this personalization is limited to the content of the Fiori catalogs for which the user is authorized.

To define the launchpad groups, perform the configuration described in the following steps:

- Create the group.
- Add tiles to the group from configured catalogs (see Figure 2.6).

Figure 2.6: Example of a group

2.4.3 Front-end roles

SAP roles are used to assign Fiori catalogs and Fiori groups to users. Using SAP roles, you manage what tiles the user has access to (catalogs), what tiles the user sees by default (groups), and what tiles the user can execute (profiles) in the Fiori launchpad. You use the SAP role maintenance transaction PFCG to create these (tile) roles.

To define PFCG roles for Fiori tiles, perform the following steps:

- Create the PFCG role on the central gateway hub.
- Assign one or more catalogs to the menu part of the role (see Figure 2.7).
- Assign one or more groups to the menu part of the role (see Figure 2.7).
- Generate the profile from the authorizations part of the role.
- Assign the role to the user.

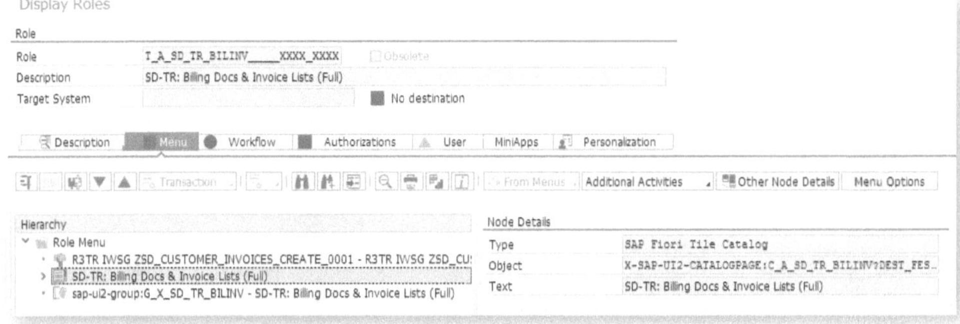

Figure 2.7: Catalogs and groups in the role menu

A user with a particular tile role assigned will see the intersection of what is implemented within the assigned catalogs and groups displayed in their Fiori launchpad when they log on.

2.4.4 Back-end roles

As a final step in authorizing tiles in Fiori launchpad, we have to assign the catalogs to an SAP role on the back end. This will ensure that the necessary services are also available in the back-end system. You can also enter the services manually in the role, but referencing is the better option.

To define PFCG roles for Fiori tiles on a NetWeaver back-end system, perform the following steps:

- Create the PFCG role on the NetWeaver back-end system.
- Assign one or more catalogs to the menu part of the role (see Figure 2.8).
- Generate the profile from the authorizations part of the role.
- Assign the role to the user.

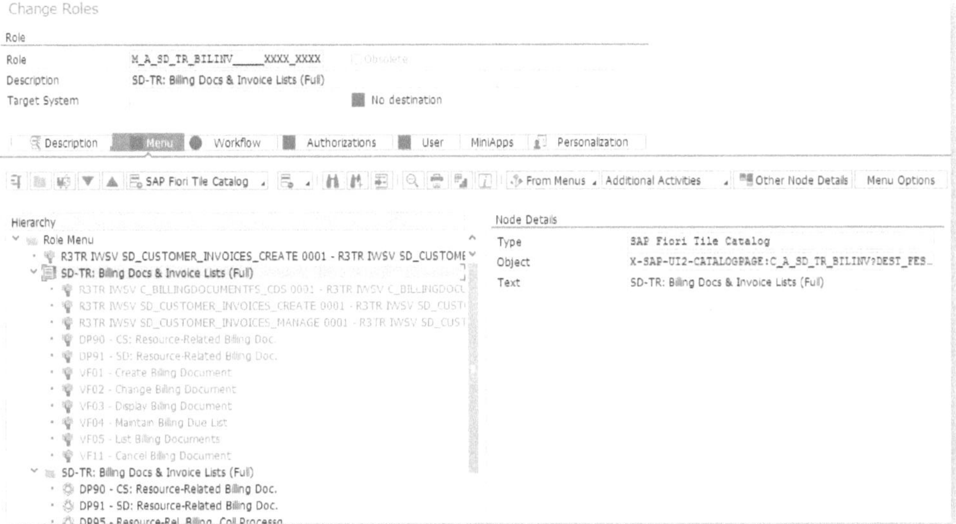

Figure 2.8: Catalogs in the role menu of a back-end role

2.4.5 Key authorization objects

In addition to the entries in the role menu, you need specific authorizations on the central hub to allow a connection to a back-end system via trusted RFC and to be able to consume the OData services on the front-end server. Moreover, specific authorizations on the back-end systems are required to connect back to the front-end server and to consume the OData services on the back-end server.

The following authorization objects are essential when creating tile roles on the central hub and on any NetWeaver back-end system:

S_SERVICE

This authorization object is automatically checked when external services are started. From a security perspective, it must be interpreted as the S_TCODE authorization object for external services. The same restriction considerations as for S_TCODE should be applied to S_SERVICE.

The Profile Generator automatically assigns authorizations if an external service is entered in a role menu (see Figure 2.9). The S_SERVICE authorization object contains two fields:

- SRV_NAME: Hash value of the external service
- SRV_TYPE: Type of the external service

Standard Check at Start of External Services S_SERVICE
Standard Check at Start of External Services T-G191044201
Program, transaction or functi 3AE0F596EBE1843EC6B22737ED90F6, 4CC78858CF7211088AB530E1E00F95 <...> SRV_NAME
Type of Check Flag and Authori HT SRV_TYPE

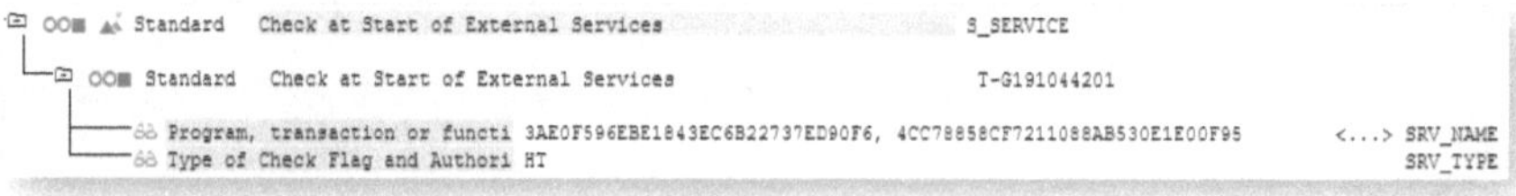

Figure 2.9: Example of an S_SERVICE authorization

S_RFC

This authorization object is checked when SAP function modules are connecting to SAP systems through *Remote Function Calls (RFC)*.

The authorization objects contain three fields (see Figure 2.10):

- ACTVT: allows execution (value 16) of the RFC
- RFC_TYPE: possible types are function group (FUGR) and function module (FUNC)
- RFC_NAME: the name of the function group or function module

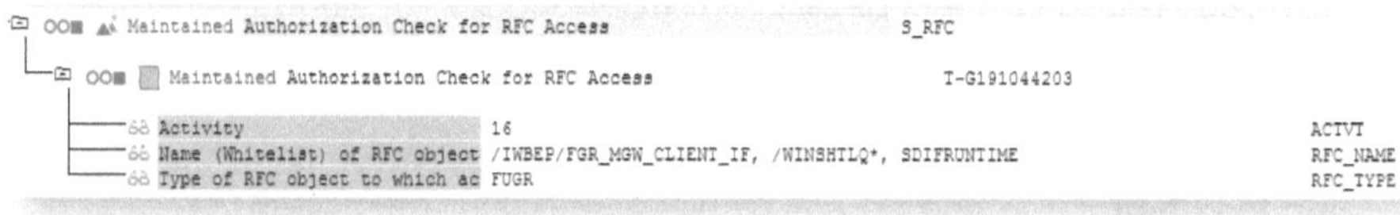

Figure 2.10: Example of an S_RFC authorization

S_RFCACL

This authorization object is checked when RFC users connect to trusted systems through Remote Function Calls (RFC).

The authorization objects contain seven fields (see Figure 2.11):

- ACTVT: allows execution (value 16) of the RFC
- RFC_CLIENT: client of the calling system
- RFC_EQUSER: flag that indicates whether the user can be called by a user with the same ID (Y = Yes, N = No)
- RFC_INFO: installation number of the calling trusted system
- RFC_SYSID: ID of the calling system or the domain of the satellite system
- RFC_TCODE: transaction code of the calling transaction
- RFC_USER: ID of the calling user (only needed when RFC_EQUSER is N)

Manually	Authorization Check for RFC User (e.g. Trusted System)	S_RFCACL
Manually	Authorization Check for RFC User (e.g. Trusted System)	T-G191044200
Activity	16	ACTVT
RFC client or domain	100, 500	RFC_CLIENT
RFC same user ID	Y	RFC_EQUSER
RFC information	*	RFC_INFO
System ID (for SAP and Externa	SD1, SP1, SQ1	RFC_SYSID
RFC transaction code	*	RFC_TCODE
RFC User (SAP or External)	8	RFC_USER

Figure 2.11: Example of an S_RFCACL authorization

The use of the asterisk (*)

Be very careful when using asterisk (*) values in the authorization objects described. In all cases, the field values for these objects must be adequately restricted to avoid uncontrolled breaches of your systems.

Error trapping

The traditional error-trapping tools for authorizations, such as SU53, ST01, STAUTHTRACE, and ST22, will not provide the full information on what is missing when a particular tile is not working. Executing transaction code /IWFND/ERROR_LOG will provide the necessary information, including whether the error is caused on the front-end or back-end system.

For the back-end authorizations on the target systems needed to execute transaction codes, the UI5 application, HANA views, BW reports, etc., see the specific chapters on S/4HANA, HANA, and other back-end system security for more details.

2.4.6 KPI modeler

The previous sections dealt with transactional apps for which the Fiori launchpad designer is used to create static or dynamic tiles. For *key performance indicator (KPI)* tiles, however, you have to use the *KPI modeler* to create them and to bring KPI tiles onto the Fiori launchpad. Figure 2.12 provides a schematic overview on how to set up KPI tiles. We will discuss each part in the following sections.

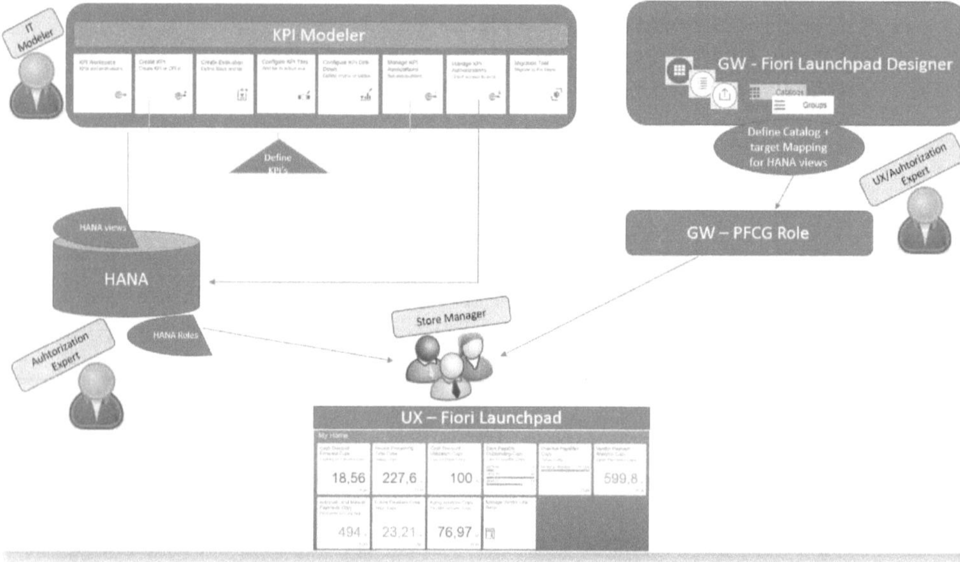

Figure 2.12: Overview of the authorization setup with the KPI modeler

KPI tiles

The KPI tiles are typically designed and implemented by an IT modeler. The following configuration steps have to be performed in the KPI modeler:

- Create the KPI. In the data source of the KPI definition, refer to the SAP HANA view and its corresponding OData service. Note in Figure 2.13 that you can define the semantic object/action here as well, but this is not mandatory. If you provide the values here, they will cascade down to the next step, which is the evaluation attached to the KPI.

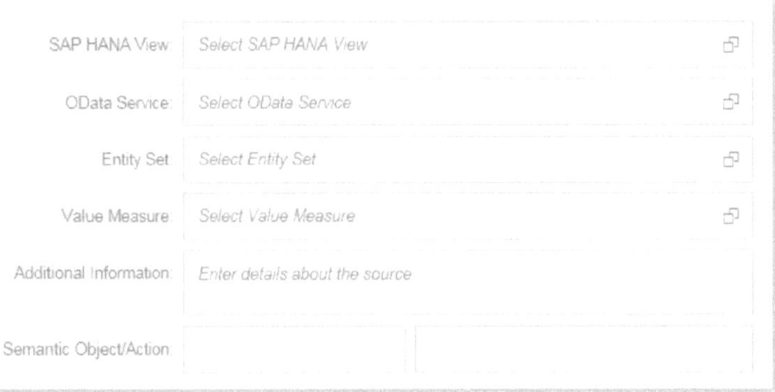

Figure 2.13: Defining the KPI

- Create the evaluation. For a new KPI, you have to create at least one evaluation—but you can also create more than one. The data source definition you provide here will be used for your reporting purposes.
- Configure drill-downs. For each evaluation, you can add a drill-down configuration. As the term suggests, this part would allow the end user to enter a drill-down visualization configured here from the analytical app. As this is an optional step, only a few analytical apps support this drill-down functionality at the time of writing this book.

- Configure the KPI tile. To bring the tile onto the Fiori launchpad, use the CONFIGURE KPI tile. For each active evaluation, attach a tile from the templates shown in Figure 2.14. Note that the semantic object/action is also provided here. It overrides the values entered in the KPI creation.

Figure 2.14: Templates for KPI tiles

In summary, you use the KPI modeler to bring a tile onto the Fiori launchpad and to display KPI-related information on the tile. The Fiori launchpad uses the active evaluation assigned to the KPI tile to trigger the XSOData/query to retrieve the results from the HANA database. Once the KPI tile has been rendered on the Fiori launchpad, the users can click the tile to navigate to the target app. This navigation is governed by the semantic object/action which is configured above.

HANA roles

Once you have configured the KPIs, you have to assign them to an SAP HANA role so that the user can see them in the Fiori launchpad. To do this, perform the following steps:

- Create a HANA role containing the access to the KPI views.
- Create a HANA role authorizing the KPI runtime.

- Create a composite HANA role containing the above two single roles.
- Link the composite HANA role to the KPIs in the KPI modeler.
- Assign the composite HANA role to the user in SAP HANA.

Front-end roles

HANA roles alone are not sufficient. On the front end, you will need to provide access to the target mappings that have been used during the configuration of the KPI tiles in the KPI modeler. Access to the target mappings are granted through Fiori catalogs. Tiles will not be configured in the Fiori launchpad designer as the tiles were configured in the KPI modeler. Perform the following steps:

- Create a Fiori catalog in the Fiori launchpad designer.
- Configure the necessary target mappings in the catalog.
- Create a Fiori group in the Fiori launchpad designer. This group will be empty at this point in time, as the group will be completed by the KPI modeler.
- Create a front-end role in PFCG.
- Assign the catalog and the group to the menu part of the role.
- Create a KPI runtime role (needed during runtime in the Fiori launchpad).
- Generate the profiles from the authorizations part of the roles.
- Assign the roles to the user, either directly or by using a composite role.

2.5 Conceptual considerations

Now that we know the technical details and the generic steps for granting access to Fiori applications, it is decision time again. Indeed, you will have to decide on the structure, the content, and the naming conventions for your catalogs, your groups, and your front-end roles (tile roles). These conceptual design considerations will be discussed in the following sections. We have already discussed how this front-end setup ties up with your back-end roles in Section 1.4.

2.5.1 Fiori catalogs

As mentioned earlier in this chapter, Fiori catalogs are a collection of apps or tiles that determine what an end user has access to in the Fiori launchpad. This means that, when building Fiori catalogs, you have to decide what tiles you will put together considering what the end user should be allowed to access. This exercise is quite similar to the grouping of transaction codes into PFCG roles on a back-end system.

It is good practice to define and document the criteria you will apply for structuring your catalogs and for separating certain tiles into separate catalogs. In fact, it is essential that these criteria are always applied, not only during the implementation phase, but also during the support phase.

Important considerations when establishing the criteria for the grouping of tiles into catalogs are:

- Long-term sustainability: When setting up Fiori security, the goal is not only to have an optimal concept at the end of the implementation phase and at the time of go-live; you need to ensure that your original setup remains in the same optimal shape in the months and even years after the go-live. The quality of your grouping criteria and the way these are respected at all times are essential to the long-term sustainability of your security setup.
- Transparency: The design of your Fiori catalogs determines what the end user will have access to in the Fiori launchpad. The quality of the catalog design will contribute to the Fiori experience for the end user. On the other hand, the catalogs must be transparent for the technical people maintaining the catalogs. Consequently, transparency in structure and naming convention, both from a technical and a business perspective, must be achieved.
- Consistency: When you click a tile in the Fiori launchpad, some back-end functionality is triggered (on S/4HANA, on HANA itself, or on any other back-end system). Any errors in this process are highly undesirable and the opposite of the user experience SAP is aiming for. In other words, the front-end setup must be 100%

consistent with the corresponding back-end authorizations. If a user has access to a certain tile in the Fiori launchpad, you must ensure that the related back-end functionality is adequately authorized as well.

We are convinced that the criteria for designing catalogs is highly dependent on the way you design your back-end roles. In fact, back-end and front-end roles (including catalogs and groups) should be considered together to create a coherent cross-system concept.

2.5.2 Fiori groups

Fiori groups determine what an end user sees by default in the Fiori launchpad. A user might have access to more tiles in the launchpad (based on the catalogs), but the groups determine the default set of tiles visible at logon. Consequently, Fiori groups are an important design element in determining the default view the end user sees at logon.

While the Fiori catalogs have a strong relationship with the back-end authorizations (the tiles have to work on the front end and the necessary back-end authorizations have to be available as well), the Fiori groups focus more on cosmetics. Because the groups determine what the user sees by default, the following considerations are important for grouping tiles:

- Screen layout: Every authorized Fiori group will result in a separate heading in the Fiori launchpad with a set of tiles underneath. Decisions on the granularity of the Fiori groups will consequently have a direct impact on the presentation on the screen.
- Default tiles: Determining what apps and tiles are mostly used is an important consideration. Typically, you would want to include the commonly used apps and tiles in the Fiori groups so that they are visible to the end user by default. You can opt to include only the more specific apps, only those used on occasion, or only those used by specific users in the authorized catalogs so that the end user can search for them in the Fiori launchpad and include them in their personalization scope.

2.5.3 Fiori front-end roles

Fiori front-end roles or tile roles are collections of Fiori catalogs and/or Fiori groups that are used to assign the catalogs and groups to the end user.

Important considerations here are:

- Consistency between front end and back end: When you assign a set of apps and tiles on the front end to an end user, you must make sure that you also assign the correct related back-end authorizations. These back-end authorizations must be complete (all apps and tiles need to work correctly) but not excessive. The good old principle of segregation of duties and the granting of authorizations on a need-to-have basis still apply on the back-end systems. Having this all matched up between the systems is indeed the main challenge.
- Ease of assignment on front end and back end: When an end user needs access to your landscape, it must be reasonably easy for a user administrator to determine what roles to assign on the different systems. If no identity management functionality is available, this might present another challenge. Conceptual transparency and strong naming conventions might be a big part of the solution.

2.5.4 Back-end roles

The back-end roles are discussed in Chapter 1 of this book. It must be clear that cross-system consistency is becoming more and more important. Our ideas for a state-of-the-art, cross-system authorization concept are discussed in Chapter 1, tying all the authorizations on the different systems in your landscape together.

3 Securing SAP HANA

After discussing the S/4HANA and Fiori security in the previous chapters, in this chapter we focus on the HANA database security. As SAP HANA allows you to work directly in the database when modelling or consuming views, security must be considered not only from the application layer point of view but also from the database point of view.

It is really important to secure the database because it holds all the tables used in the application layer. If HANA access is not secured, all data can be read and altered directly from the database! Therefore, security consistency is really important. Having a good security concept on the application layer is important but the database must also be secured to be properly protected.

In the following, we discuss the specific HANA authorizations mechanisms and how they can be applied in a sustainable authorization concept.

3.1 Implementing HANA security

SAP HANA security is managed differently to SAP ABAP security. There are no transaction codes and authorization objects in HANA—instead, there are privileges.

We will now discuss the user types, privileges, and method of grouping the privileges in order to secure an SAP HANA system.

3.1.1 User type

In SAP HANA, there are no parameters to define the user type like there are in the ABAP layer. All users are database users. However, we can distinguish between *database users* and *internal database users*.

Database users

To be able to log on to HANA, you must have a user in the *HANA identity store*. Database users are created by the administrator and correspond to real persons. They can be deleted, and, in that case, all objects owned by and privileges granted to that user are deleted too!

There are two types of database users: *standard users* and *restricted users*.

▶ Standard users

Standard users can log on to HANA with either an ODBC/JDBC connection or an HTTP/HTTPS connection. They can create objects in their own schema. The standard PUBLIC role, allowing consumption of some system views, is automatically granted to them (see Figure 3.1).

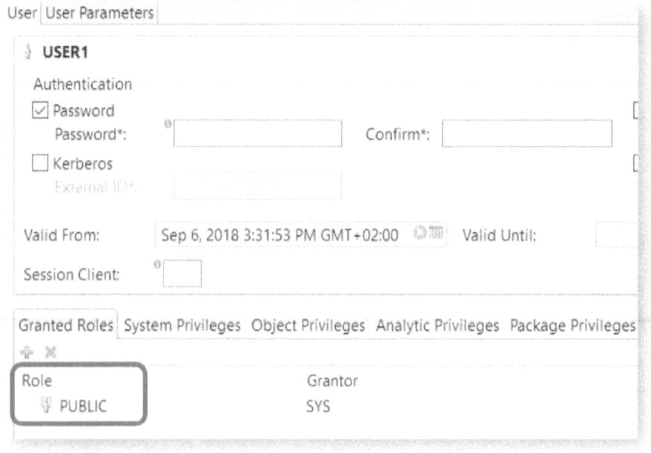

Figure 3.1: Standard user

▶ Restricted users

Restricted users can initially log on to HANA only via an HTTP/HTTPS connection. They cannot create any objects in their schema and have no automatically assigned privileges (see Figure 3.2).

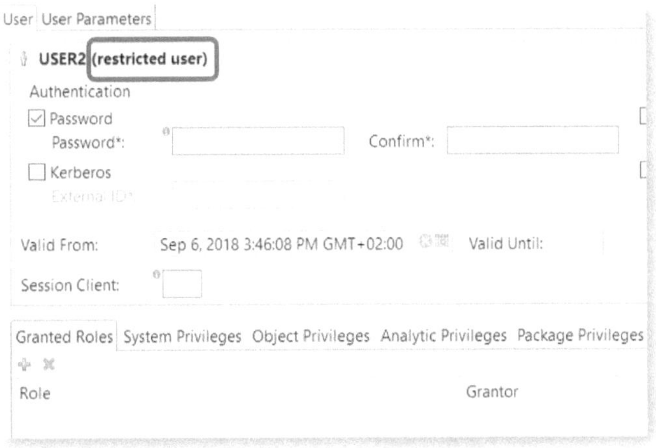

Figure 3.2: Restricted user

There is no button or command to easily convert a database restricted user into a standard user. However, restricted users can be granted the possibility to use an ODBC/JDBC connection and be allowed to create objects in their own schemas.

Internal database users

Internal database users are **not real users but technical users**. Most of them are created when a system is installed and they cannot be deleted. As they cannot be deleted, everything they own and have created remains in the system. Therefore, these users are used for administration tasks.

Furthermore, logon is not possible with most internal database users. The following users are examples of internal database users: SYS, _SYS_REPO, _SYS_STATISTICS.

The SYSTEM user is an exception as it can be used to log on. That user is meant to be used for the initial setup to create the first roles and users and should then be deactivated.

User type summary

Table 3.1 below recapitulates the main differences between the database users and the internal database users:

User	Properties
Database user	Real user Can be deleted If it is deleted, all objects it owns are deleted and all privileges granted to the user are deleted
Internal database user	Technical Cannot be deleted For most of them: no logon possible Main usage: for administrative tasks

Table 3.1: HANA user type properties

3.1.2 Privileges

Authorizations in HANA are based on privileges. There are five types of privileges:

- System privileges
- Application privileges
- Package privileges
- Object privileges
- Analytic privileges

As shown in Figure 3.3 and Figure 3.4, these five categories of privileges are always visible in roles or users.

Figure 3.3: HANA privileges from the user point of view

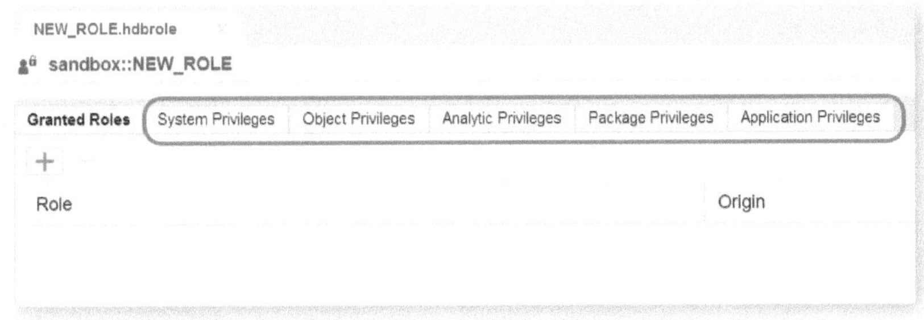

Figure 3.4: HANA privileges from the role point of view

The first four types of privileges provide functional restrictions, whereas the last type, the analytic privilege, provides organizational restrictions.

In contrast to the other privileges, which can be assigned to roles or users, note that for users only, there is an additional type of privilege: the *privileges on users*.

We will look at the details of each type of privilege below.

System privileges

System privileges apply to the entire system and are mainly used for administrative purposes.

They are valid across the system and cannot be altered. In a multitenant database, system privileges apply only in the database where they are granted to users. The only exception is with the DATABASE ADMIN system privilege. This privilege, granted in the system database, allows operations on the tenant databases (e.g., create and drop tenants).

System privileges can be divided into five sub-categories:

- Users and role management

Example: USER ADMIN, which allows the creation, alteration, and deletion of users

- Catalog and schema management

Example: CREATE SCHEMA, which allows the creation of schemas

- Auditing

Example: AUDIT ADMIN, which allows the creation and maintenance of audit policies and the audit configuration

- System management

Example: BACKUP ADMIN, which allows the definition and creation of backups and recoveries

- Data import and export

Example: IMPORT, which allows the import of data into the database

Application privileges

Application privileges apply to the XS applications, that is, the applications running on the HANA XS engine.

These privileges should be used in addition to the other required privileges for the application (system privilege, object privilege, etc.) and they are created by the XS application developers. Some granularity for accessing the different parts of an application is feasible (e.g., accessing the landing page, accessing a particular screen within the application, etc.). This allows a granular authorization approach by providing only the required application privileges to the users based on their functions and what they have to access within the application.

Package privileges

Package privileges apply to the packages within the SAP HANA repository.

These privileges are used to define the access to repository packages and the authorized activities on the design-time objects within those packages. In HANA, the packages hold the design-time version of objects such as views, procedures, roles, etc. The package privileges work with a hierarchal logic, which means that a privilege granted on a higher package will automatically be inherited for all of its sub-packages.

The highest package is the root package, REPO_PACKAGE_ROOT. Therefore, any access granted on that root package is inherited to all packages.

The system checks the user's authorization for the package when the user tries to execute an operation. If the check fails, the system checks the authorizations on the higher package in the hierarchy chain, right up to the root package.

For package privileges, we distinguish between *native packages* and *imported packages*. Native packages are created in the system in scope. Imported packages are created in another system and then imported into the system in scope. In a typical infrastructure with development, quality, and production environments, design-time objects are created in a native package within the development system. The package and its content are then transported to the quality environment for testing and, after validation, to the production environment. In the quality and production environments, that package is an imported package, whereas in the development environment, it is a native package.

Updates should not be executed within imported packages unless this is required for emergency modifications.

There are four types of package privileges:

- REPO.READ

Allows read access to the package (native or imported) and all its design-time objects.

- REPO.EDIT_NATIVE_OBJECTS/
REPO.EDIT_IMPORTED_OBJECTS

Allows the creation and editing of design-time objects within a native or imported package.

- REPO.ACTIVATE_NATIVE_OBJECTS/
REPO.ACTIVATE_IMPORTED_OBJECTS

Allows the activation of design-time objects within a native or imported package.

- REPO.MAINTAIN_NATIVE_OBJECTS/
REPO.MAINTAIN_IMPORTED_OBJECTS

Allows the update, deletion, or creation of new sub-packages within a native or imported package.

Object privileges

Object privileges apply to database objects such as schemas, tables, procedures, etc. but also to design-time objects in the SAP HANA repository such as views.

Object privileges are used to define the access to the objects and allow modification of those objects. Depending on the object type (e.g., a schema, a view, a procedure, etc.) different activities can be granted, such as SELECT or INSERT for a view, EXECUTE for a procedure, etc.

As schemas hold other objects, all authorizations granted on a schema level are automatically inherited to all the objects contained in that schema.

The system checks the user's authorizations for the object on which the user tries to execute the action. If the check fails, the system checks the authorizations on the schema which holds the object as schemas are objects containing other objects. This means that a user can display a table without having a SELECT access to that table but by having a SELECT access to the schema which holds the table.

Analytic privileges

Analytic privileges apply to views and allow you to control what values or combination of values a user can see within a view. This is the privilege type that should be used for organizational restrictions.

Analytic privileges can be used with attribute views, analytic views, and calculation views.

Analytic privileges always contain the following restrictions:

- Model restrictions
  - Determine which view the privilege is used for
  - Can involve one or more views
- Activity restrictions
  - Determine the activity which is authorized on the view
  - Only one activity per analytic privilege is allowed
  - All analytic privileges are currently automatically restricted to the READ activity as calculation, attribute, and analytic views are read-only views

- Validity restrictions
  - Determine the analytic privilege's validity period

Other attribute restrictions can be added based on the fields available within the view (e.g., company code, plant, etc.). They specify the values to be displayed for those fields.

The values within the attribute restriction can be **static** or **dynamic**. Static values are a combination of a logical operator (e.g., equal, between, etc.) and a static value (e.g., 100, plant01, etc.). Dynamic attribute restrictions are a combination of a logical operator (e.g., IN) and a stored procedure in order to determine the filters to be applied for the selected models. The filters are then determined at runtime. The analytic privilege is then called a *dynamic analytic privilege*.

Any one analytic privilege can have one or more attribute restrictions and a combination of both static and dynamic attribute restrictions. If no attribute restriction is entered in the analytic privilege, the system automatically adds all attributes which will allow the user to see all data within the view. Also, if no values are specified for a defined attribute restriction, the system automatically adds all values, which will allow the user to see all values for that specific attribute.

There are two types of analytic privileges:

- XML analytic privileges
  - Also called *classical analytic privileges*
  - They are XML based and can be created with the graphical interface

- SQL analytic privileges
  - They are SQL based and can be created with the graphical interface or the SQL editor

Table 3.2 summarizes the main properties of both types of analytic privileges.

Property	XML analytic privilege	SQL analytic privilege
Applicable to tables	No	No
Applicable to analytic views	Yes	Yes
Applicable to attribute views	Yes	Yes
Applicable to calculation views	Yes	Yes
Applicable to SQL scripted calculation views	No	Yes
Can be created with the SAP HANA Studio or the Web-based workbench (= SAP HANA classic XS environment)	Yes	Yes
Can be created with the SAP Web IDE for SAP HANA (= SAP HANA XS advanced environment)	No	Yes
Is transportable	Yes	Yes
Can include complex filtering	No	Yes

Table 3.2: Properties of the types of analytic privileges

Therefore, the main differences between the two types of analytic privileges are that SQL analytic privileges allow more complex filtering logic and that they are also compatible with SQL scripted calculation views and with the new HANA XS Advanced environment. For those reasons, SAP recommends working with SQL analytic privileges instead of XML analytic privileges.

How do you migrate XML analytic privileges to SQL analytic privileges?

You can use the migration tool within SAP HANA Studio to migrate your XML analytic privileges to SQL analytic privileges.

Each view can be either defined without security or secured with XML analytic privileges (called *Analytic Privileges* in the view's properties) or SQL analytic privileges (see Figure 3.5).

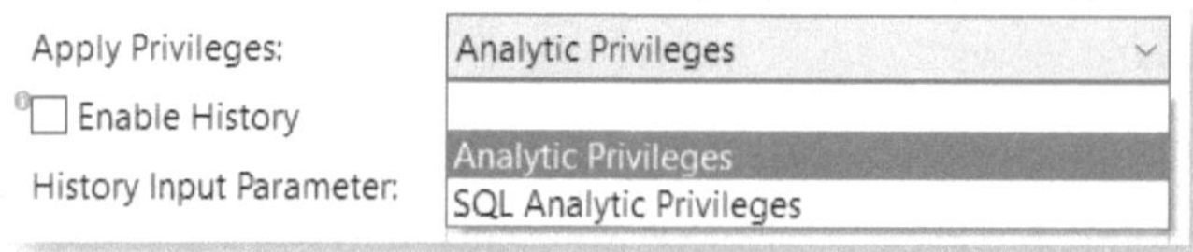

Figure 3.5: Security applied to a view

If the view is defined without any privileges applied, the system only checks whether the user has access to the view. The access can be either with a SELECT statement on the view itself or on the schema which contains the view. If the user has access to the view, all of the view's data is displayed.

If the view is defined with privileges applied, the system checks whether the user has access to the view, either with a SELECT statement on the view itself or on the schema which contains the view. The system also checks whether the user has the related analytic privilege. Depending on what has been defined in the view's properties, the privilege will be either an XML or an SQL analytic privilege. If the user has both access to the view and the corresponding analytic privilege, the view's data is displayed based on the conditions defined in the analytic privilege.

Pay attention to the authorization check type defined in the views!

Per default, *XML Analytic Privileges* is selected in views but this can be switched to *SQL Analytic Privileges* if required! One view cannot be defined with both XML and SQL analytic privilege authorization checks simultaneously.

- Dynamic analytic privileges

Dynamic analytic privileges are XML-based or SQL-based analytic privileges which refer to a stored procedure in order to determine the filters on a view dynamically at runtime.

Stored procedures used in dynamic analytic privileges must be read-only, executable by the user _SYS_REPO, and defined in DEFINER mode. DEFINER mode means that the security checks for the procedure execution are executed on the privileges of the owner of the procedure, which for a repository procedure is always _SYS_REPO.

Watch out with dynamic analytic privileges!

In the event of an error during the execution of the procedure which is part of the dynamic analytic privilege, the user receives a NOT AUTHORIZED... message, even if he has the correct analytic privileges for displaying the data!

- Filters and restrictions: Logical combinations

Multiple analytic privileges are combined with an OR operator. Within an analytic privilege, multiple attribute restrictions are combined with an AND operator. Within an attribute restriction, multiple value restrictions are combined with an OR operator.

Example:

If you have two analytic privileges, AnalyticPrivilege1 and AnalyticPrivilege2, they are combined with an OR operator. This means the less restrictive privilege is applied.

Within AnalyticPrivilege1, the different attribute restrictions are combined with an AND operator.

Within each attribute restriction of AnalyticPrivilege1, all the restrictions are combined with an OR operator.

The example above is summarized in Figure 3.6.

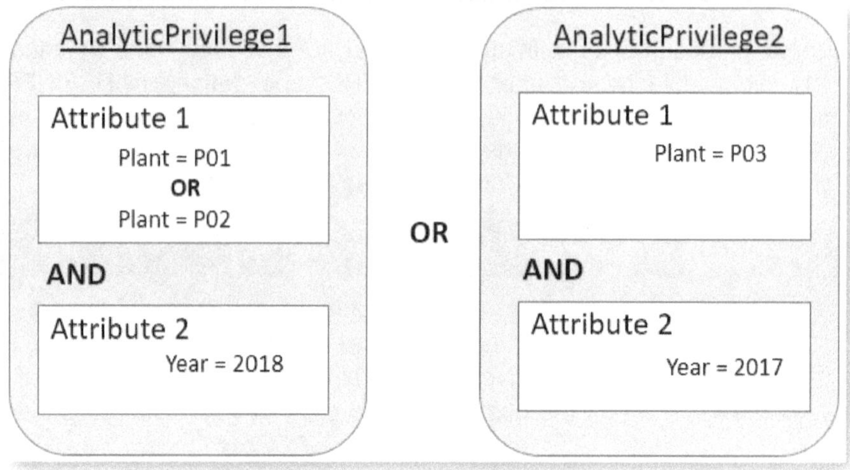

Figure 3.6: Logical combinations of analytic privileges

Within AnalyticPrivilege1, attribute 1 will generate the following restriction: (Plant = P01) OR (Plant = P02) and attribute 2 will generate the following restriction: Year = 2018.

The combination of both restrictions within AnalyticPrivilege1 on attribute 1 and attribute 2 will generate the following restrictions: ((Plant = P01) OR (Plant = P02)) AND (Year = 2018).

Within AnalyticPrivilege2, the combination of both attribute 1 and attribute 2 will generate the following restrictions: (Plant = P03) AND (Year = 2017).

A user having both AnalyticPrivilege1 and AnalyticPrivilege2 for the same view will have the following WHERE clause for that view: (((Plant = P01) OR (Plant = P02)) AND (Year = 2018)) OR ((Plant = P03) AND (Year = 2017)).

User privileges

Only one privilege can be granted to a user—the ATTACHED DEBUGGER privilege. This privilege allows another user to debug SQL script code in the user in scope's session.

In addition to being granted that privilege, the user debugging the SQL script code also needs DEBUG privilege on the objects to be debugged.

Note that this privilege can only be granted to a user by the user in scope himself.

3.1.3 Roles

Privileges can be grouped into roles. There are two types of roles within HANA:

- Catalog roles, which are runtime roles
- Repository roles, which are design-time roles

Catalog roles

Catalog roles are roles which have been created immediately as a runtime object and which only exist as such. They are owned by the role creator and they cannot be transported.

Repository roles

Repository roles are created as design-time objects and their runtime versions are created automatically by the system at activation time. Repository roles are owned by a technical user, _SYS_REPO, which is also the owner of all the repository content as well as the activated version of the roles. Repository roles can be transported from one system to another.

Catalog roles vs repository roles

Table 3.3 summarizes the main properties of both types of roles.

Property	Catalog role	Repository role
Role ownership	The owner is the role creator. Therefore, when the creator is deleted, the role is deleted.	The owner is a technical user (_SYS_REPO) which can never be deleted.
Role creation	The system privilege ROLE ADMIN is required to create new catalog roles.	An EDIT access on a package in the repository is required to create a new repository role within that package.
Addition of objects to role	The role creator must have a privilege in order to add that privilege to a role.	Any objects owned by the technical user _SYS_REPO can be added to the role.
Transitiveness	If a privilege is removed from the role creator, the privilege is automatically removed from the catalog roles he has created.	There is no relation with the role creator's privileges but if a privilege is removed from _SYS_REPO, it is removed from the repository roles.
Role versioning	There is no versioning possible with catalog roles.	There is a version management system which is available for repository roles.
Role assignment	Only the role creator can grant the role or someone who has the role with the option GRANTABLE TO OTHER USERS AND ROLES flagged.	Any user with the authorizations to execute the stored procedure GRANT_ACTIVATED_ROLE can grant any repository role to any user.
Role revocation	Only the grantor of the role can revoke it.	Any user with the authorizations to execute the stored procedure REVOKE_ACTIVATED_ROLE can revoke any repository role from any user.

Property	Catalog role	Repository role
Transport	Catalog roles cannot be transported between systems. They have to be created at runtime in each system.	Repository roles can be transported between systems using the HANA transport mechanism.

Table 3.3: Properties of HANA role types

3.2 Conceptual considerations

Now that we have seen the technical HANA security specifications, we will discuss how to translate these into a strong and sustainable HANA security model.

3.2.1 Determining the HANA security required

Different architecture scenarios are possible with SAP HANA and the method of direct access to the HANA database will determine the security required.

If neither the IT department (except the database administrator) nor the business is accessing the HANA system, no specific security is required. This is the case, for example, when the regular database has been migrated to a HANA database and the end users only access the application layer (e.g., ABAP S/4HANA). The communication between the application layer and the HANA database goes through a technical user (see Figure 3.7).

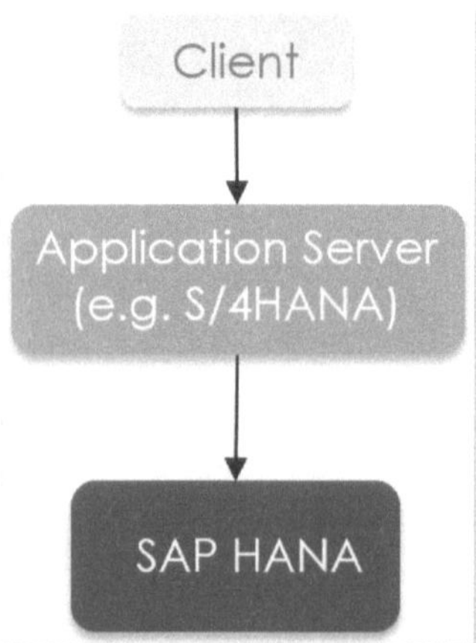

Figure 3.7: Landscape architecture: no direct access to HANA

If at least some end users or the IT department (e.g., the modelers) need to access the HANA database directly to consume data or perform IT tasks, HANA security is required in addition to the application layer security (see Figure 3.8).

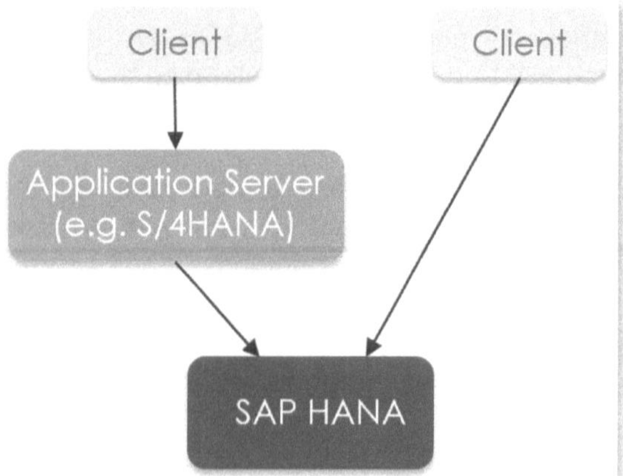

Figure 3.8: Landscape architecture: direct access to HANA

3.2.2 User type

As we have seen, only database users can be created. Within that user type, standard users are intended for IT persons (database administrator, security administrator, modelers, etc.) as they can use an ODBC/JDBC connection. In contrast, restricted users are intended for business users as they can connect via client applications only (HTTP/HTTPS access).

However, some reporting tools use an ODBC/JDBC connection. Therefore, either business users are created as restricted users, then enabled for ODBC/JDBC connection, granted the required roles for ODBC/JDBC access, the PUBLIC role, and are authorized to create objects in their own schema if required; alternatively, business users are immediately created as standard users.

Furthermore, in SAP HANA there is only a user ID, no first or last names. Therefore, the recommendation is to have a strong user ID naming convention and, if possible, to use the same user IDs as in the application layer.

3.2.3 The SYSTEM user

The SYSTEM user is created with some powerful privileges to create users and roles at the time of installation and for system management purposes. This user should therefore not be used for daily activities and especially not in the productive environment. Once the installation is complete and the initial users and roles have been created, allowing them to perform their activities (e.g., user and role creation), the SYSTEM user should be deactivated.

3.2.4 Catalog objects ownership

All catalog objects created by a user are owned by this user, as well as all privileges the user has granted to others or to catalog roles. This is because the action of granting privileges is also considered as an object which is owned by the user who has executed this action (see Figure 3.9).

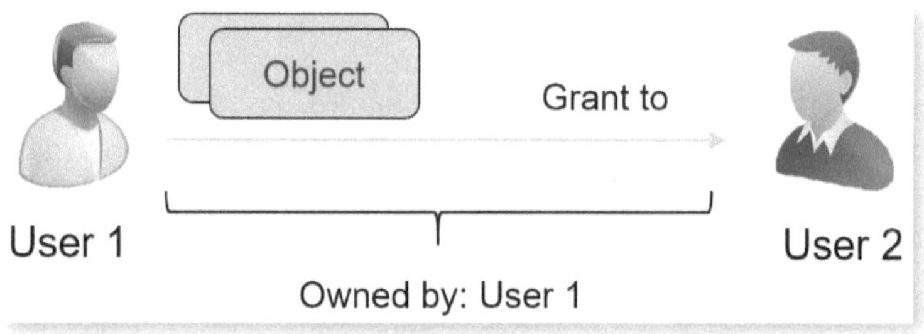

Figure 3.9: Catalog object ownership

Object owner deletion time

When a user is deleted, everything owned by that user is deleted. Thus, all objects built on top of the deleted objects become corrupted as the data source on which they are based no longer exists.

If the owner of a schema is deleted, all objects in the schema are also deleted, even if they are owned by a different user. All privileges on these objects are also deleted.

As a precaution, when you try to delete a user, the HANA system will offer two options (see Figure 3.10):

- RESTRICT
  If the system detects any dependent objects linked to the user, neither the user nor the objects will be deleted
- CASCADE
  Even if the system detects dependent objects linked to the user, both the objects and the users will be deleted anyway

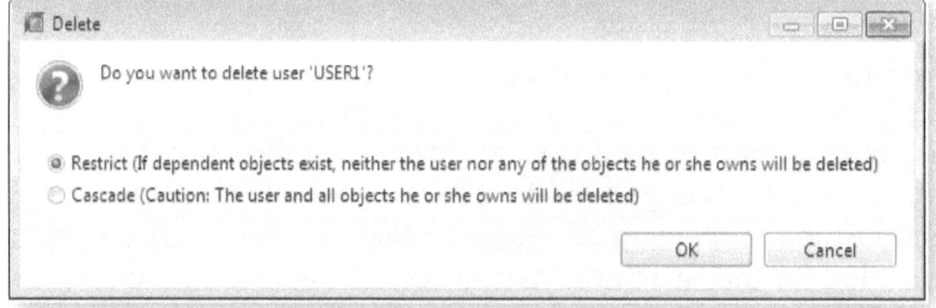

Figure 3.10: User deletion mode

The recommendation is to use the RESTRICT option to ensure that nothing important is lost when the user is deleted and to stop a deletion if any valuable objects would be lost (e.g., schema, table, etc.).

Note that even in RESTRICT mode, only the schema content owned by the user is visible, not the objects granted by the user (e.g., catalog roles or privileges granted to catalog roles or directly to users) for which the granted action will be revoked.

Be careful when deleting a user!

When you delete a database user, all objects created by that user, as well as all privileges granted to others by that user, are also deleted.

Use an appropriate object owner

Therefore, when you create schemas or tables under an exposed view, you should use a database user acting only as a technical user instead of the modeler's regular user IDs. The goal is to ensure that the creator of such catalog objects, who is also the owner of those objects, is not deleted. Note that we do not recommend using the SYSTEM user as this user should be deactivated after system installation.

A clear naming convention should be established for database users used as technical users to ensure they are always easily identified and thus never deleted.

How do you avoid accidental loss of data?

To avoid accidental loss of data, when creating catalog objects below exposed views, use an easily identified, dedicated user which will never be deleted.

3.2.5 Repository objects ownership

Repository objects (e.g., views created in the repository, repository roles, etc.) are always owned by the internal database user _SYS_REPO. This user cannot be deleted therefore there is no risk of losing data if the creator of a repository object is deleted.

3.2.6 Granting the initial access to an object

Initially, access to an object can only be granted by the owner of the object or of the schema where the object is located.

If the object has to be used by a user other than its owner, access to the object must be granted to this other user. This user can be a database user or, for repository objects, the internal database user _SYS_REPO.

Because not all schemas are used below models, the user _SYS_REPO does not automatically have privileges for all schemas. This means that if information from a specific schema is used in a model, _SYS_REPO must be granted access to that schema.

Furthermore, if _SYS_REPO has to grant access to that object to another user (e.g., via a repository role), _SYS_REPO must have access to it **with grant option**. This means that _SYS_REPO not only has access to the object but can also grant access to it to any other user. This is done via the following SQL syntax which can only be executed by the schema owner:

```
GRANT <activity. e.g. SELECT > ON SCHEMA <schema name> TO
_SYS_REPO WITH GRANT OPTION
```

3.2.7 Authorization checks for objects

Authorization check on objects without dependencies

When objects have no dependencies, meaning that they do not rely on any other object, the authorization check is only performed on the object itself. So, the user trying to access the object needs only:

- The relevant privilege on the object itself

Hence, to execute a function or a procedure, an EXECUTE operation on the function or procedure or an EXECUTE operation on the schema which holds the procedure or the function is required.

However, as activated versions of repository objects are included in the schema _SYS_BIC, granting an EXECUTE operation on that schema is not recommended as not only the procedure or function in scope would be accessible, but all other repository procedures and functions as well!

Authorization check on objects with dependencies

- Definer mode

When the objects (e.g., procedures or views) are based on other objects and have been created in definer mode, the authorization check is executed on the rights of the person/user who created the object. In that case, there are two conditions which must be met to access the object:

- The user accessing the object must have the relevant privilege on the object itself
- The object creator must have the relevant privileges on all underlying objects and must be authorized to grant those privileges to others

In the case of repository objects (e.g., procedures or views) based on other objects, this means that _SYS_REPO must be authorized for all those underlying objects and must be granted the possibility to grant those objects to others. If not, only the owner of the object and nobody else will be able to access the object.

- Invoker mode

If the object is created in invoker mode, the authorization check is executed on the user accessing the object. In that case, the two conditions to be met to access the object are:

  - The user accessing the object must have the relevant privilege on the object itself
  - The user accessing the object must have the relevant privileges on all underlying objects

When you create a procedure, it is therefore very important to decide whether to do so in definer mode or in invoker mode. Views are automatically created in definer mode—except for SQL scripted views, for which you can define the SQL security mode!

Particular object: Secured views

To access a secured view, a SELECT operation on the view or on the schema which holds the view is required, together with the corresponding analytic privilege.

You should avoid granting a SELECT operation on the whole _SYS_BIC schema which contains all activated views for business users as all views will be accessible unless they are secured. In that case, the view will be visible for the end user but when they try to consume the data, an **unauthorized** error message will be displayed. Business users should only see the views they are allowed to access.

- Independent views

For secured views which are not based on other column views, the system will only check whether the user is authorized to access that view and has the required analytic privilege.

- Dependent views

For secured views with dependencies, the system will check whether the user is authorized to access the exposed view and has the required analytic privilege linked to it and also the privileges for all the secured views below this exposed view. This means that things can become quite complex very quickly!

Figure 3.11 shows all the views and tables below one exposed view with dependencies.

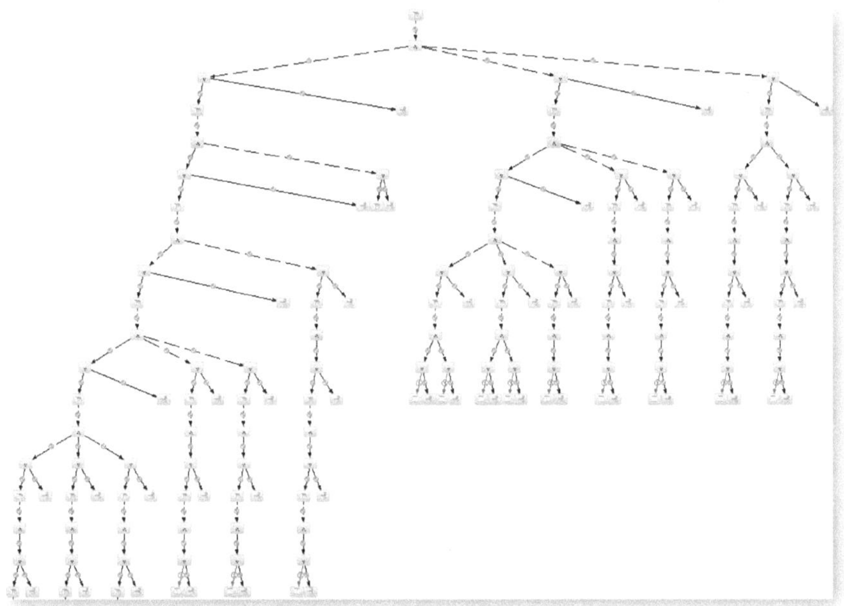

Figure 3.11: Example of HANA view dependencies

Therefore, the best practice is to have only the exposed views secured with analytic privileges and all underlying views unsecured as they will never be accessed directly by the end users (see Figure 3.12). This implies that access to the view should be granted by a SELECT operation on the view itself and the corresponding analytic privilege. The views below this level should not be secured and access to them should be granted only to _SYS_REPO (with grant option), which is automatically the case for all the repository views.

As views are either secured or not secured, a view cannot be simultaneously exposed, and therefore secured, as well as below another view, and therefore unexposed, where it must be unsecured.

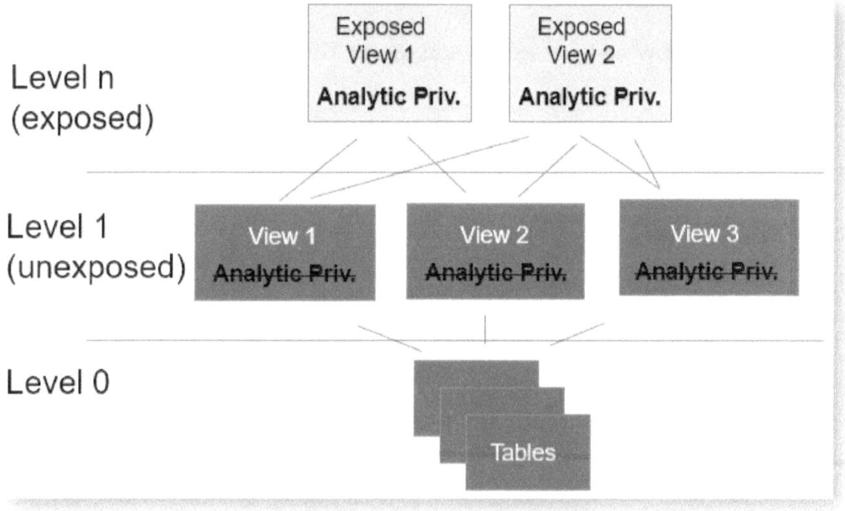

Figure 3.12: Concept for securing HANA views

Therefore, the end user will see only the exposed views, but note that not all calculation views are visible with the reporting tools. There are three types of data category within calculation views and only the cube data category type is visible in the reporting tools, not the dimension or default data category.

Analytic privilege logic

When a secured view with an analytic privilege is consumed, the data is returned based on the conditions of the analytic privilege.

In an analytic privilege, the APPLICABLE TO ALL INFORMATION MODELS checkbox will make the restriction applicable to all views that have that field (e.g., COMPANY CODE), even if they are not part of the models of the analytic privilege. Therefore, this checkbox should be used with caution as it removes the flexibility to have different attribute restriction values for different views.

Also, when executing a query on a view which returns values the user is not authorized to display, SAP HANA returns only the values authorized for the user. No error message regarding the unauthorized values is displayed, in contrast to the situation in SAP BW. Therefore, the user may think there are no values for that query whereas there are, but the user is just not authorized to see them!

▶ Analytic privilege for multiple views

SAP HANA specifies attribute names (field names) in a different way for attribute views than for analytic views and calculation views.

For attribute views, the attribute name is defined via <package _hierarchy>/<view_name>$<attribute_name>.

For analytic and calculation views, the attribute name is only defined via its name: <attribute_name>. There is no link to a specific view within the analytic privilege.

Therefore, if one analytic privilege contains multiple attribute views, a distinction can be made between each view and its filtered attributes, whereas this cannot be done for analytic and calculation views as the attributes do not contain a link to the view to which they apply within the analytic privilege. In that case, the attribute is applied to all views within the analytic privilege.

As a consequence, all attributes to be restricted for analytic and calculation views within one analytic privilege must have exactly the same name (including lower and upper case specification) otherwise there will be a problem when the analytic privilege is activated. Attribute names are case sensitive and if one of the views within the analytic privilege does not have the field, the system will return an error message saying that the field does not exist.

For example, if an analytic privilege contains multiple views and the restricted field is COMPANYCODE and this field is included in all views, the restriction on that attribute is applied to all those views. However, if that field is written COMPANYCODE in one view and COMPANYCODE (i.e., all in lower case) in another view within the same analytic privilege, it will not be activated.

- _SYS_BI_CP_ALL

There is one broad analytic privilege that is applicable for all views secured with classical analytic privilege (XML analytic privileges): _SYS_BI_CP_ALL. This analytic privilege contains no restrictions at all and therefore provides full access to all data from the views secured with classical analytic privileges. Of course, this analytic privilege will overrule any other analytic privileges the user has for a view. This is why it should not be granted to business users.

Note that the analytic privilege _SYS_BI_CP_ALL only works for XML analytic privileges—there is no equivalent for SQL analytic privileges!

Use _SYS_BI_CP_ALL with caution!

As the analytic privilege _SYS_BI_CP_ALL overrules any other classical analytic privilege and gives unrestricted data access within views, be very careful who you grant this privilege to!

- Dynamic analytic privileges

The advantages of using dynamic analytic privileges is that one analytic privilege can provide different output for different users. The logic within the dynamic analytic privilege can be complex and the dynamic analytic privilege requires less maintenance as it refers only to the stored procedure. However, the tables to which the stored procedure refers must be maintained.

The disadvantages of dynamic analytic privileges are that to report on the users' access, not only do the analytic privileges held by the users have to be checked, but also all the tables that the stored procedures within the dynamic analytic privileges refer to have to be checked as well. Over the long term, it's easy to forget one table. Furthermore, if those tables are maintained by the business, the Security Officer is not the only one granting access in the system and if there is an approval mechanism in place for access requests, it is important to ensure it also applies to those tables.

Note that dynamic analytic privileges are slower than static analytic privileges in the query process. Therefore, dynamic analytic privileges should be created carefully to limit their impact on system performance.

3.2.8 Entity relationships

In SAP HANA, the privileges can be granted directly to users or grouped into roles.

Even if technically feasible, granting privileges directly to users is not recommended as that way of working is not sustainable with a large number of users. It is also not transparent as there is nothing which indicates why a user has been given a specific privilege.

Furthermore, if the privilege is granted with the GRANTABLE TO OTHER USERS AND ROLES option selected, as shown in Figure 3.13, the receiver of that privilege can grant it to any other user or role! The Security Officer loses control of the security model as he is not the only one who can grant access rights/privileges. Plus, only the person granting access rights/privileges can remove them and, in that case, even the Security Officer won't be able to remove them!

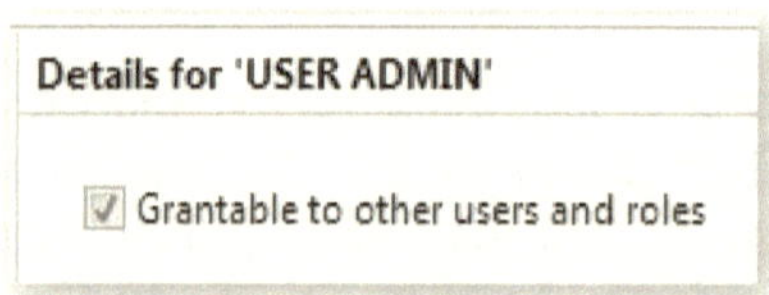

Figure 3.13: Privilege granted directly to a user and grantable to others

Be careful with directly assigned privileges!

If the GRANTABLE TO OTHER USERS AND ROLES option is selected for a privilege, the user can grant the privilege to any other user or role and thus the Security Officer loses overall control of his security model!

Alternatively, the privileges can be grouped into roles. However, the roles can also be granted directly to users or grouped into other roles. Unlike in the ABAP application layer, in SAP HANA there are no single and composite roles. This means that a role can contain privileges but also other roles. Furthermore, a role can contain another role which also contains another role, etc.

The possible entities relationship between privileges, roles, and users can be summarized as shown in Figure 3.14.

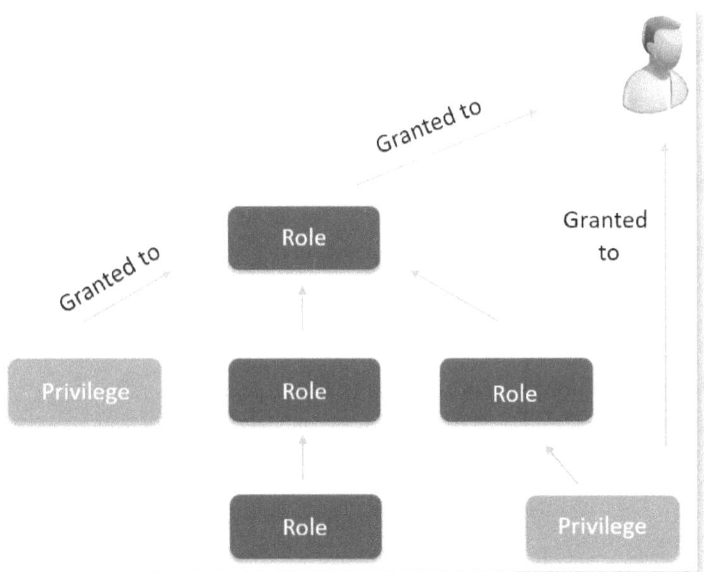

Figure 3.14: Relationships between privileges, roles, and users

3.2.9 Roles

The role concept will represent the required functional and organizational restrictions. It should be maintainable and transparent.

Role concept

Even if SAP HANA allows you to have multiple layers of roles in roles, we recommend that you mimic the two-layer concept generally used in the ABAP application layer. This concept uses a first layer of roles, called *single roles*, which group access based on tasks. The concept then uses a second layer of roles, called *composite roles*, which contain the task roles and which are based on the business functions (see Figure 3.15).

The transparency is obtained because the accesses are grouped logically together for each task and are not assigned alone, but also because those tasks are grouped together within business functions. This structure clearly shows why a user has been given a particular access.

The maintainability comes from the fact that when a task requires a new access, the access only has to be given at the task single role level and it will be inherited by all users sharing a composite role that includes that task. Also, if a task is to be removed from a particular business function, removing it from the composite role impacts all users assigned to that function simultaneously. There is no need to remove that task from each user individually.

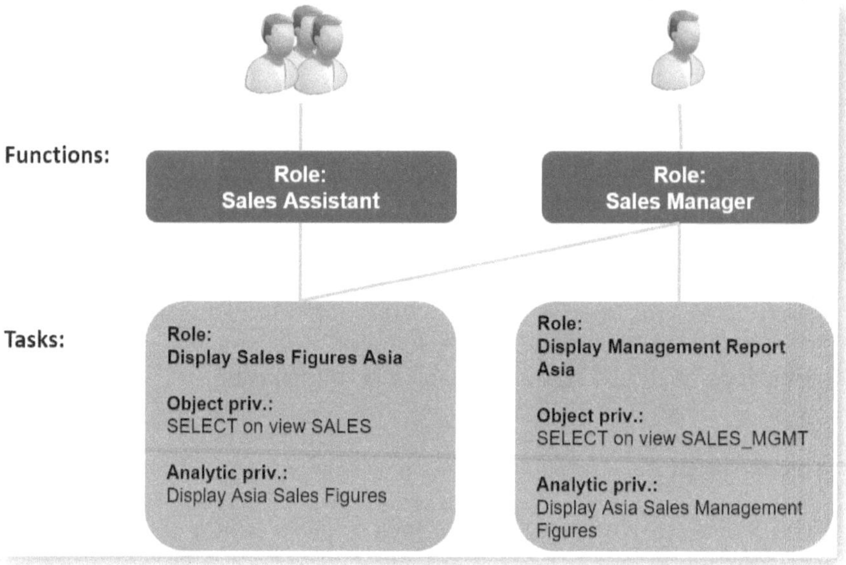

Figure 3.15: Two-layer role concept for HANA

Role type

We recommend that you use only repository roles, and never the catalog roles.

Indeed, due to the properties of catalog roles, as discussed earlier, to create a catalog role you would need to have all privileges assigned to you in the production environment as catalog roles are not transportable.

Furthermore, the roles could be deleted if their owner, which is the person who created them, is deleted, or the privileges could be removed from the role if they are removed from the access granted to the person who created the role.

Also, in the same way as for privileges, if a catalog role is granted with the GRANTABLE TO OTHER USERS AND ROLES option selected, the receiver of that role can grant it to any other user or role (see Figure 3.16)! The Security Officer is therefore not the only one granting access rights! Furthermore, only the person granting access can remove it, so in that case, the Security Officer won't be able to remove the access!

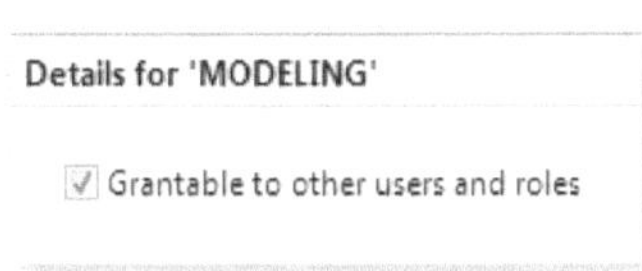

Figure 3.16: Catalog role granted to user and grantable to others

Be careful with catalog roles grantable to others!

If the GRANTABLE TO OTHER USERS AND ROLES option is selected for a catalog role, the user can grant the role to any other user or role and thus the Security Officer loses overall control of his security model!

In contrast, using repository roles allows you to create roles in a development environment, have them tested, and then transported up to the production environment. Furthermore, the person creating the role does not need to have all the privileges they want to grant in the role as only the internal database user _SYS_REPO has all these privileges. This means that it is important to give access to _SYS_REPO with the grant option to any catalog objects beneath an exposed model or which should be granted to any user via a repository role. Also, because the owner of the role is the user _SYS_REPO, the Security Officer can grant or revoke any repository role.

With repository roles, you can achieve a split between the role creator (which can create the role in the development environment), the role owner, and the role assigner.

Pay attention to the role type when creating a new role!

When you create a new role from the security node within the HANA Studio or the Web interface, it is a catalog role which is created. Creating a repository role is less obvious—you have to do this from the content node within a package!

Because repository roles are owned by the internal database user _SYS_REPO, they cannot be directly assigned by the Security Officer. The Security Officer has to execute a stored procedure which involves the technical user _SYS_REPO assigning the role to the end user. The stored procedures for granting and revoking roles are:

- GRANT_ACTIVATED_ROLE
- REVOKE_ACTIVATED_ROLE

As the assignment is performed by _SYS_REPO, that is the name which is indicated as being the grantor of the role to the user. Thus, an audit policy should monitor the use of those two procedures.

Identify who has assigned or revoked repository roles

Create an audit procedure to identify who has assigned and revoked repository roles to/from users.

Note that the stored procedures GRANT_ACTIVATED_ROLE and REVOKE_ACTIVATED_ROLE can be copied and edited—for example, to allow roles to be assigned and revoked only from a specific package. This allows you to have some granularity within the function which can assign and revoke roles to users, which can be useful if some roles are very sensitive. In that case, however, the new procedures can only be called via SQL syntax. Role assignment via SAP HANA Studio or Development Workbench graphical interface will not work with the newly developed procedures.

3.2.10 Types of privileges required by IT and business users

Typically, an IT user, such as a system administrator, a Security Officer, or a modeler, will need the following types of privileges:

- System privileges
- Application privileges
- Package privileges
- Object privileges
- Analytic privileges

A business user will need the following types of privileges:

- Application privileges (if required)
- Object privileges
- Analytic privileges

Of course, the privileges should be assigned not directly to users but rather grouped in different roles and then the roles assigned to users.

3.2.11 Cross-database authorizations in a multitenant environment

In a multitenant architecture, users or views can access data from a table or a view in a remote tenant from their own system. The access is a read-only (SELECT) access. In a multitenant database environment, each tenant has its own set of users, isolated from the other sets, and therefore a mechanism of remote identities is used.

Consider an SAP HANA system with a system database and two tenants. The tenant in which the user is logged on, runs a query, and sees the results is called the target database. The tenant where the source of the data is located is called the source database.

In the target database, the user can query a view which exists in the source database (see Figure 3.17) by executing the following SQL syntax in that target database:

```
SELECT * FROM "<source DB>"."_SYS_BIC"."view1"
```

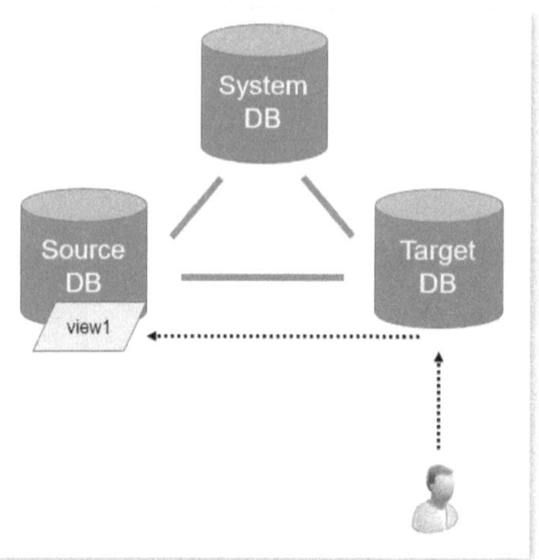

Figure 3.17: Multitenant database query

This means that a user in the target database will be associated with a user in the source database, which is the remote identity. Hence, part of the query is executed by that remote identity located in the remote source database. Therefore, the remote identity must have sufficient privileges to access the data source as the authorization check in the remote database is performed on that user (the remote identity).

Alternatively, as shown in Figure 3.18, the user can query a view in the target datbase which is based on source data residing in the source database by executing the following SQL syntax in that target database:

```
SELECT * FROM ”_SYS_BIC”.”view2”
```

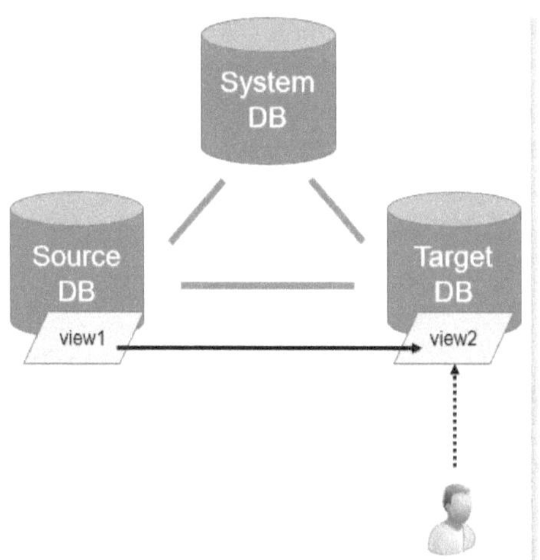

Figure 3.18: Multitenant database views

This means that a user in the target database does not need a remote identity in the source database. However, the internal database user _SYS_REPO does need a remote identity in the source database as it needs to access the source data. Furthermore, as _SYS_REPO is activating repository objects, this user must be able to grant access to others.

As each tenant has its own set of users, both _SYS_REPO users are completely independent and isolated from each other. Furthermore, the _SYS_REPO users cannot be defined as each other's remote identities. Therefore, a dedicated user should be created in the source database and linked to _SYS_REPO in the target database. The dedicated user needs the required access on all source database tables and views which are below the target database views. The user also needs to have the **with grant option** in order to allow _SYS_REPO in the target database to activate the view and grant access to it to other users. As the dedicated user should be used only for that purpose, it can be granted a SELECT operation with grant option on the schema _SYS_BIC in the source database.

Note that remote identities are unidirectional and that a user can be defined as a remote identity of only one user in another tenant. A remote identity can only be defined via an ALTER USER SQL statement. It cannot be defined via the SAP HANA Studio graphical interface or via the

Web-based security workbench interface. As the user sets in each tenant are independent of one another, if a user is deleted in one tenant, the remote identities of this user will remain in the other tenants and will have to be deleted there manually. Finally, remember that when you check a user's access in a specific database, the access the user has in remote databases via his remote identities are not included in the results!

3.2.12 Troubleshooting authorization issues for view access

A couple of tools are available for troubleshooting HANA authorization issues:

- Views
- Authorization dependency graphical interface
- Trace

Views

The main view for troubleshooting authorization issues for a specific view is EFFECTIVE_STRUCTURED_PRIVILEGES. For a specific user, it will show:

- The privilege applicable to a particular view and the filter condition
- Whether the user is authorized to see the view or not
- Whether the views below this view are secured or not

This will indicate whether the user in question is missing any privileges.

Of course, other views such as ACCESSIBLE_VIEWS, which lists all accessible views for a specific user, EFFECTIVE_PRIVILEGES, which indicates all privileges assigned to a particular user, or EFFECTIVE_ROLES, which details all roles assigned to a specific user, may also be helpful.

Authorization dependency graphical interface

The *authorization dependency viewer* is an SAP HANA Studio tool which displays the dependencies for objects with complex dependencies, such as calculation views and stored procedures, graphically.

The tool shows the objects and all dependent objects below them in a hierarchical tree (see Figure 3.19). If one object is used multiple times in different places, it will appear in each place. The type and color of the line between each object indicates the nature and status of the authorizations between those objects. A solid line indicates an OR connection between the parent node and the child nodes, which means authorization is required on only one of the child nodes. A dashed line indicates an AND connection between the parent node and the child nodes, which means authorizations are required on all child nodes. With regard to the color of the line, if the user has an invalid authorization for one of the underlying objects, a red line is used, whereas a black line is used when the user is authorized.

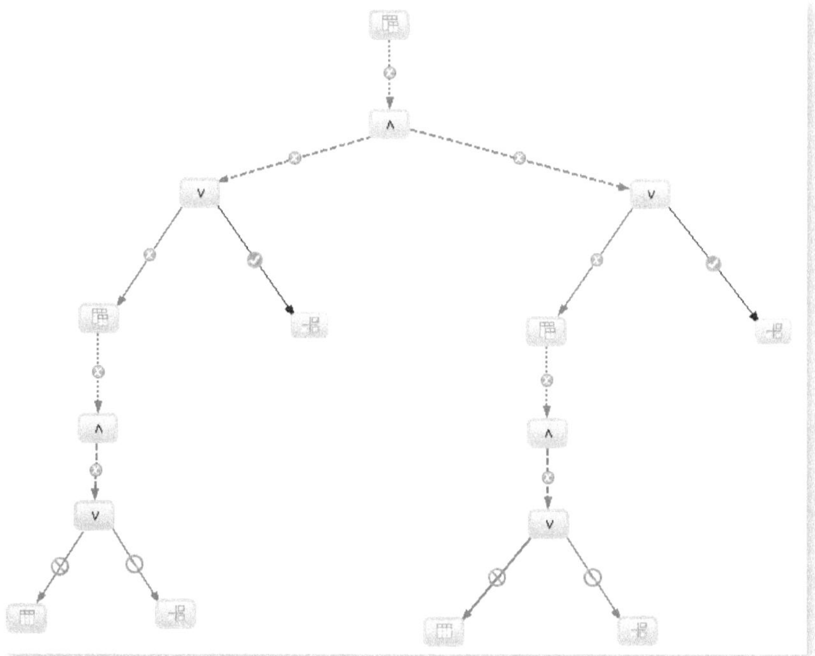

Figure 3.19: Authorization dependency viewer

Invalid authorizations occur when the object owner has neither the required privileges on the object nor the authorization to grant them to others.

Therefore, invalid authorization can occur because:

- The user does not have the privilege for the underlying object (SELECT for views, EXECUTE for procedures, etc.)
- The user has the privilege for the underlying object but cannot grant the privilege to others (**with grant option** is missing)
- The user has the privilege for the underlying object but cannot grant the privilege to others because it cannot be granted to others at all
- The underlying object is invalidated

For views and procedures which must be accessible to others, this graphical interface is useful to ensure that the internal database user _SYS_REPO has access **with grant option** to all underlying objects and can therefore grant access to other users to allow them to consume or execute the objects. This diagram helps you to quickly identify the missing privilege and grant it to the owner of the object, which is _SYS_REPO for repository objects.

Note that this tool will work with objects in definer mode, as in this case, it will quickly show whether the user _SYS_REPO is missing access to any underlying objects. It will not work with objects in invoker mode as in that case, the authorizations check for underlying objects will be performed on the user accessing the exposed object.

You can access this tool by right-clicking the activated version of the view or procedure which is located in the _SYS_BIC schema and then selecting SHOW AUTHORIZATION.

Tracing authorization issues

The SAP HANA system comes with different traces. From a security point of view, the main traces are the *SQL trace* and the *user-specific trace*. To configure the trace, you need the system privilege TRACE ADMIN.

The SQL trace records the SQL statements executed for either the entire set of users or for a specific database or application user. A couple of additional options are available to restrict the trace to specific tables or views, or the application or statement type.

The user-specific trace records the SQL statements executed for a specific database or application user through the different SAP HANA components (index server, name server, etc.).

Displaying the authorization components in the trace

In the user-specific trace, you must select the SHOW ALL COMPONENTS checkbox in order to be able to see the authorization component!

All trace files are visible under DIAGNOSIS FILES within the SYSTEM ADMINISTRATION section in HANA Studio or within the TRACE section of the SAP HANA Web-based development workbench.

This concludes our chapter on HANA security. After discussing the front-end security, with the S/4HANA and Fiori security, and the back-end security within this chapter, in the next chapter we will look at the question of system security.

4 Securing the infrastructure

In the previous chapters, we discussed securing S/4HANA, SAP Fiori, and the SAP HANA system. We presented our recommendations and methodology based on our experience in implementing a bulletproof security and authorizations strategy. In this chapter, we focus on securing the SAP application server, the database, the operating system, and the network infrastructure.

The Basis administrator plays a very important role in securing and hardening the SAP system. This person has a complete overview of all the different technical components and how they interact with each other. However, the administrator needs help, as the days of one person knowing everything are long gone. System technology has become too complicated. Input is needed from experienced system, database, and network administrators.

System security should be included in the high-availability and disaster recovery plans of the organization as it has an equal impact on:

- **Stability**: changes to the system should not introduce unexpected or intermittent failures
- **Availability**: strive for a 100% uptime
- **Recoverability**: consider the recovery point and time objective set by business
- **Reliability**: the system constantly performs as it is expected to
- **Resiliency**: the system should be resilient to both internal and external attacks. Most organizations focus on external attacks. However, statistics show that internal attacks are at least as dangerous and more likely to occur.

A good security implementation strategy should be ready for constant change. SAP systems and their operating environment change constantly. The strategy should therefore take the following best practices into account:

- The strategy should be the same for production and non-production. Any change to security settings should be tested on non-production systems first.
- Changes should be documented and included in easy-to-follow deployment procedures.
- Changes should not be implemented ad-hoc. Avoid firefighting as changes that are not thought through may cause instability.
- Complete an initial assessment of the current state and plan frequent evaluation assessments.

IT environments are complex. So where do you start and how do you make sure that nothing is forgotten? The security matrix in Figure 4.1 can be used as a guideline.

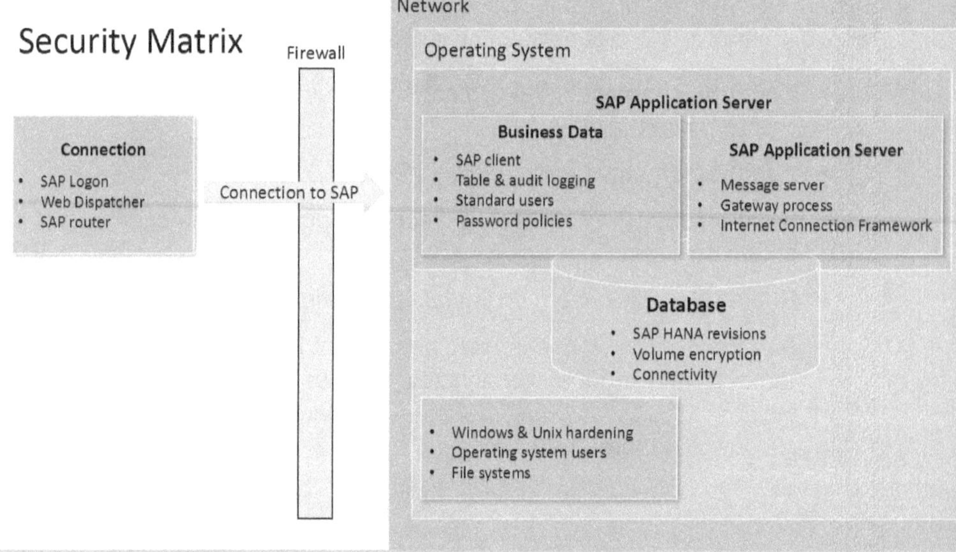

Figure 4.1: The SAP security matrix

It lists the following components which should be considered in a top-down security strategy:

- Data centers and servers
- Network vulnerabilities
- Operating system
- SAP HANA database
- SAP application servers
- Communication between systems, applications, and databases via Remote Function Calls, Web services, or file transfer
- User logons, access to system accounts

4.1 Securing the application server

SAP NetWeaver is the basis of all ABAP-based SAP applications, such as SAP S/4HANA, SAP ERP, SAP BW, and many others. From a security perspective, this is both an advantage and a disadvantage. As the underlying technology is the same for all components, a security risk in one component is likely to occur in all of them. Fortunately, the same applies for any countermeasures.

If access to your SAP solutions is needed from mobile devices, the SAP Fiori front-end server has to be hardened. This hardening exercise is vital if the server has to be accessed from untrusted devices or networks. Although there is an unstoppable trend to have data access available from any device from anywhere, data theft is still more likely to occur from inside the company than from outside. This implies that system hardening must be looked at from both an external and an internal point of view. Fortunately, most if not all hardening steps applicable to the front-end server can and should be applied to the back-end server as well.

In this section, we will list and explain the crucial hardening steps applicable to both the front-end Fiori and back-end S/4HANA system. We strongly recommend that sufficient time be planned in the implementation project to review and implement these steps. Implementing them at a later stage is unwise, as extra testing might be needed.

4.1.1 The message server

The *message server* is a very important work process within the SAP system. It informs all instances belonging to the same SAP system of each other's existence and status. It is also responsible for load balancing the clients, such as SAP Logon and RFC communication. When an instance of a system is started, it connects to the message server to register the services it provides (dialog, background, update, spool). Every 300 seconds, the message server connects to every instance belonging to the system to query the performance statistics and if necessary, to update the load balancing in favor of the system with the best performance. The message server notices if an instance fails and redirects users to another available instance. Again, this is based on the best performance. If the failed instance returns and reconnects, it is added to the load balancing pool and reconsidered again.

The message server can be monitored from within the SAP system with the *message server monitor* (transaction SMMS). It can also be monitored from within an Internet browser by connecting the HTTP port of the message server (set via the parameter ms/server_port_<xx>). In addition, it can be accessed from the operating system by calling the command MSMON or MSPROT.

The message server is a single point of failure. If it stops working, it must be restarted as soon as possible to make sure that the SAP systems keep on operating without any errors. It should therefore be protected against unauthorized access.

This protection can be accomplished with the following security measures:

- Restrict access to the message server via the external monitoring tool MSMON. Use parameter ms/monitor to restrict access. When it is set to *0*, only application servers can make changes to the internal memory of the message server and execute monitoring functions. Access via the operating system tool MSMON is disabled.
- Use parameter ms/monitor in combination with ms/admin_port. Setting ms/monitor to *1* enables access via MSMON. With ms/admin_port, you can set a port number through which an external client can log on to perform administration tasks in the message server.

- Separate internal and external communication. To prevent unwanted clients pretending to the message server that they are application servers, use the profile parameter rdisp/msserv _internal = <no.>. When this is set, the standard message server port which is set by sapms<SID> can only be used by read-only queries such as load distribution information.
- Enable SAP message server logging. This can be accomplished via profile parameter ms/audit. More information will be written to the message server trace file depending on the trace level set. Tracing has a range of 1 up to 3.
- Use an access control list for the application servers. You can use parameter ms/acl_info to point to a file. This file must include the host name, IP address, and if necessary, subnet mask of all the application servers allowed to connect to the message server. This file does not affect external clients that only want to retrieve information from the message server—this is still possible. The entries in the file must respect the following syntax; HOST = Host name or IP address or domain. For example, HOST = SAPAPPL01, SAPAPPL02 means that only logons from the application servers SAPAPPL01 and SAPAPPL02 are allowed.

See SAP Note 821875 *Security settings in the message server* for more information.

Which SAP profile? Default or instance?

The layout and the configuration of the SAP system are determined by parameters. These reside in the SAP profiles on the operating system and are read at instance startup. Parameters applicable to the SAP system, such as the initial logon client, should be set in the default profile. Parameters only applicable to one SAP instance, such as memory and process layout, should be set in the instance profile.

Which transaction? RZ10 or RZ11?

Parameters can be set from within the SAP system via transaction RZ10. It is a very straightforward transaction that performs a consistency check when a parameter is set or saved. Most parameters are static, meaning that the SAP instance has to be restarted to activate the new setting. Some parameters are dynamic. You can easily check the parameter type via transaction RZ11. You can also use this transaction to change dynamic parameters. Remember that parameters set via transaction RZ11 fall back to their default when the SAP system is restarted. Setting or changing the parameter in the SAP profiles via transaction RZ10 can avoid this.

4.1.2 The gateway process

SAP is a business application which communicates with other business applications, both SAP and non-SAP applications. Communication is via Remote Function Calls (RFC). ABAP programs can execute RFCs from the SAP system or via external programs to the SAP system. RFC is also used internally, between SAP processes of an SAP instance or an SAP system, or between SAP systems. The gateway process is responsible for all external communication. Every SAP instance or application server has one gateway process. The gateway process is vulnerable to hacker attacks as it includes an implementation of the *Berkeley remote shell (rsh)* server. Rsh can be used to run commands without authentication. This is a huge security concern as these commands may be started with the authority of the SAP service user.

The steps to hardening your SAP gateway server include the following:

Close access to the gateway process

Parameter gw/acl_mode can be set to disable access to the gateway process from untrusted systems and networks. When this parameter is set, external applications will no longer be able to connect. This is a little harsh as SAP is not a standalone application. Parameter gw/acl_mode must therefore be combined with the parameter gw/acl_file. Parameter gw/acl_file points to a file on the operating system. The file entries list networks and systems from which communication is allowed, despite access being disabled by the parameter gw/acl_mode.

If the parameter gw/acl_file is set but the specified file is erroneous or does not exist, the gateway shuts down immediately. This is because the system assumes that somebody has tampered with the file.

The gw/acl_mode file lists the networks and systems from which communication is allowed and has the following syntax:

```
<permit|deny> <ip-address[/mask]> [tracelevel] [# comment]
```

Where:

- `Permit` permits a connection and `deny` denies a connection.
- `<IP address>`: the IP address and mask (optional)
- `<tracelevel>`: trace level with which *access control list (ACL)* hits (matches of addresses based on the subnetwork mask) are written to the relevant trace file (default value 2).
- `<# comment>`: comment lines begin with a hash sign (#).

For example:

- Permit 10.1.2.0/24 # permit client network 10.1.2.0 with umask 24
- Permit 2001:db8::1428:57ab # permit using an IPv6 address
- Deny 0.0.0.0/0 # deny the rest

The file is read from top to bottom. Inserting a `deny everything else` as the last file entry is good practice.

Disallow forwarding of requests

You can use parameter gw/prxy_info to allow or disallow the forwarding of requests from other gateways. Parameter gw/prxy_info should point to a file in which partner gateways are listed. Each line describes a permitted or forbidden connection. The line must have the following syntax:

```
P or D SOURCE=hostname DEST=hostname
```

Where:

- P or D stands for permit or deny
- SOURCE stands for the source host name
- DEST stands for the target host name

SOURCE and DEST can be set to a host name, a list of host names, IP addresses with subnet masks, or domain names. Entries must be separated by a comma.

Protect the gateway from external applications

Using parameters gw/sec_info and gw/rec_info, you can set security for external programs. Both point to a file on the operating system. Parameter gw/sec_info lists programs which can be started by the gateway. Parameter gw/rec_info lists programs which can register themselves to the gateway.

Parameter gw/sec_info can be used to prevent external programs being started. Maintaining the file secinfo in the data directory of the gateway instance can prevent any unauthorized starting of external programs. The entries in this file have the following syntax.

```
USER=<user>, [PWD=<pwd>,] [USER-HOST=<user_host>,] ...
HOST=<host>,TP=<tp>;
```

Where:

- USER refers to the SAP user
- PWD is optional; the password must be supplied when calling the external program
- USER-HOST: the host from which the user can call the external program. This parameter is optional. If it is not set, the user can call the external program from any SAP instance.
- HOST: the target host

For example:

```
USER=ADMIN, PWD=pass, USER-HOST=SAPSERV01, HOST=SAPSERV02,
TP=ZBACKUP;
```

The administrator (SAP user ADMIN) can start external program ZBACKUP on SAPSERV02 when connected on the gateway from host SAPSERV01. He has to use CPIC call CMSCSP to set the security password.

Another, frequently used example:

```
USER=*, USER-HOST=local, HOST=local, TP=*
```

With this entry, all SAP users can call every possible external program as long as the program resides on the local SAP system.

Parameter gw/rec_info can be used to avoid registering external programs. The parameter points to a file reginfo in the data directory of the gateway instance. If the file exists, the gateway scans for a valid entry when an external program tries to register to the application server.

The syntax of the entries in this file is as follows:

```
TP=<tp> [HOST=<hostname>] [NO=<n>] [ACCESS=<hostname,...>]
[CANCEL=<hostname,…>] [NO=<number>]
```

Where:

- `TP` relates to the name of the external application
- `HOST` equals the name of the host from which the application is connecting. An IP address or domain name can be used as well.
- `ACCESS` can be set to a domain. When set to *.company.com, the program can only be used by hosts from that domain. Access attempts from a different domain will be rejected.
- `CANCEL`: when set to a host name or domain, only those hosts or hosts from that domain may terminate a registered connection.

- `NO` equals a number. When set to a number, only that number of external programs with this name can connect. All the others are rejected.

Example:

```
HOST=* TP=BIZZTALK NO=1
```

Meaning that only one program can be registered with the name BIZZTALK. All other attempts to register a program with this name are rejected.

```
TP=*, HOST=local
```

Only external programs residing on the same host as the SAP instance can register them to the gateway.

Additional information on disabling access to the gateway is available in SAP Notes 1480644, 1444282, 1989587, and 2325191.

Configure external security

As explained above, you configure the message server and gateway process using configuration files which reside on the operating system. Maintaining these files using standard text editing tools is not recommended as these cannot intercept typing or syntax errors.

Note that the gateway process will shut down when the configuration parameters point to files which do not exist or which contain syntax errors.

To avoid syntax errors, you can maintain the configuration files from within the SAP system via transaction SMGW and the menu option GOTO • EXPERT FUNCTIONS • EXTERNAL SECURITY (see Figure 4.2). The advantage is that syntax errors are marked in **red** if the line contains errors or **yellow** if an entry in a line contains errors.

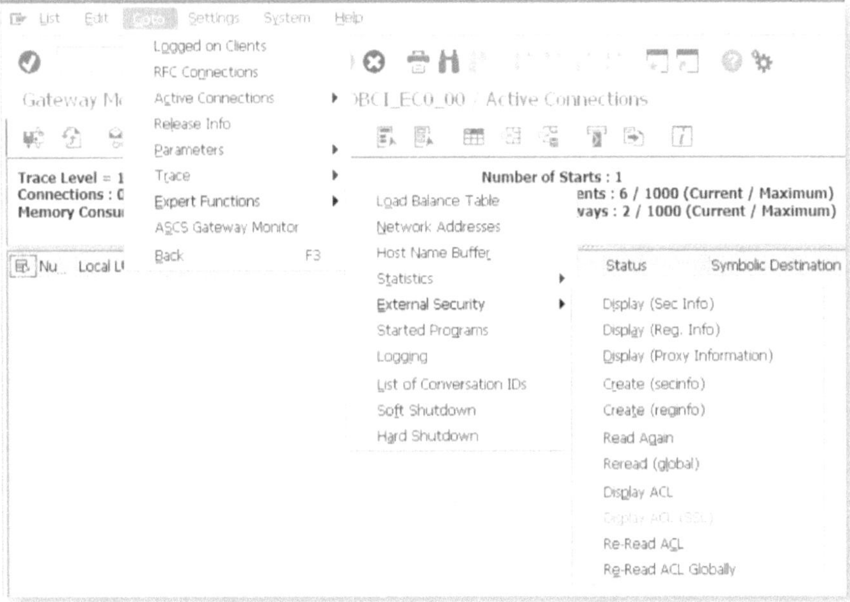

Figure 4.2: Transaction SMGW, configuration of the message server and gateway process

Additional configuration settings

Disabling or enabling the following settings can increase security even further:

- **Disable untrusted connections**: The Berkeley remote shell (rsh) is built into the gateway process. Although it is vulnerable from a security perspective, many administrators have exploited it to execute remote commands on the secondary or standby host of a high-availability cluster, for example. The gateway process can be enabled for *Secure Network Communications (SNC)*. Although SNC complicates things, it should be considered in environments with high security requirements.
- **Disable remote tracing**: With remote tracing enabled, an attacker can gather trace information from the gateway process to gain access to sensitive system data (including internal IP address information) that can be used to gain additional access. Set the

profile parameter gw/accept_remote_trace_level to *0* to mitigate the risk of disclosing sensitive data.

- **Set up logging**: Parameter gw/logging can be set to enable additional logging. All communication to and from the gateway process, the starting of external applications, and rejected connections will be logged. The content of the file can be displayed via the gateway monitor (transaction SMGW, menu option GOTO • EXPERT FUNCTIONS • LOGGING).
- **Enable RFC authorization checks**: When a Remote Function Call is executed, an authorization check is performed. The authorization check is determined by profile parameter auth/rfc_authority_check which has a range from *0* to *9* in which *0* means *Only check logon, no authorization* and *9* means *auth/rfc_ authority_check*. In production systems, the parameter should be set to *9*.
- **Avoid RFC logons with initial or expired passwords**: RFC logon will work with initial or expired passwords. This is because in contrast to SAP logon, the change password screen cannot be shown at logon. To avoid this behavior, set rfc/reject_expired_ passwd parameter to *1*. See SAP Note 161146 *RFC logon with the initial password*.

4.1.3 The Internet Communication Framework

The *Internet Connection Framework (ICF)* is an integral part of the SAP system. It is responsible for responding to HTTP, HTTPS, and SMTP requests and forwarding them to the relevant application, which consists of several ABAP programs. It is the *Internet Communication Manager (ICM)* which actually handles the requests. This is a process which runs on every SAP instance. Transaction code SMICM is used to monitor and administrate the ICM. Transaction SM51 can be used to see the details of the ICM work process.

Once you have installed *Application Server ABAP (AS ABAP)*, all Internet Communication Framework (ICF) services are available in an inactive state for security reasons. After the installation, you have to decide which services must be activated for the applications you want to use. Services can be activated or deactivated using transaction SICF. All services are displayed in a tree format that corresponds to their URL. For example, tree entry SAP • BC • GUI • SAP • ITS • WEBGUI corresponds to sap/bc/gui/sap/its/webgui, which is the URL for the SAP Web GUI.

The following security measures in relation to the ICF should be considered:

Only enable services that are really needed

In a freshly installed system, all but the essential ICF services are deactivated. Unfortunately, many SAP configuration guides will advise you to activate all services. This **activate all to avoid further configuration problems** methodology is not desirable from a system security point of view as it increases vulnerability. In addition, you end up with services being active without anybody knowing that they are active or even worse, why they are active. We therefore recommend that you only activate services which are really needed.

Disable multiple logons

This is a very old security measure which is implemented in many organizations. It avoids multiple logons with the same user ID. Users often share their user name and password—for example, because they are out of the office and need something done by a colleague, fast. They know they shouldn't do this, but they do. Accepting this behavior makes it possible for user IDs to become compromised and used to impersonate someone without this being noticed. Activating the check for multiple logons does not avoid user credentials being shared but does ensure that credentials cannot be used simultaneously, which would compromise them. Unfortunately, the parameter login/disable_multi_gui_login is only applicable to the good old SAP Logon. If you want to activate this behavior for ICF services, you have to activate the check for multiple logons on the ICF service itself.

In transaction SICF, navigate through SAP • BC• GUI • SAP • ITS • WEBGUI and then go to the ERROR PAGES • CONFIGURATION tab and enable CHECK FOR MULTIPLE LOGON (see Figure 4.3.)

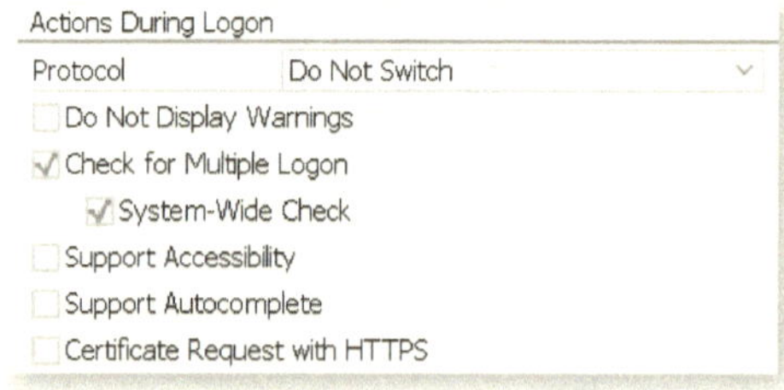

Figure 4.3: Check for multiple logons

Disable HTTP access

HTTP is vulnerable to the man-in-the-middle attack. The man-in-the-middle attack is an attack in which an attacker relays the communication between two parties. The communicating parties believe that they are communicating with each other. This allows the attacker to intercept all communication. These types of attacks might be difficult to pull off from a corporate network, but they are relatively simple in free and unsecured Wi-Fi networks. The most straightforward method of avoiding these attacks is to simply deactivate HTTP access. This can easily be accomplished from transaction SMICM by deactivating the HTTP service.

Activate HTTP security session management

When a session is ended or times out, the system ends all applications connected to this session. A session starts when a user logs on to the system and ends when the user disconnects or is disconnected by the administrator or when there is no activity and the time-out parameter is reached. Session management allows users to start another application, which normally requires a logon, without logging on again.

The following parameters impact session management and increase security:

- login/create_sso2_ticket: permits the generation of logon or authentication assertion tickets.

- login/accept_sso2_ticket: defines whether the system accepts logon and assertion tickets.
- login/ticketcache_off: logon ticket caching is used to increase the speed of the logon procedure for a specific user after that user has logged on for the first time. When disabled, the user will have to authenticate more often. This should only be considered in environments with sensitive data (for example, HR).
- login/ticket_only_by_https: when set to *1*, a session cookie will only be sent to the browser when using HTTPS. As we recommend deactivating HTTP altogether, this parameter should be considered by default.
- icf/set_HTTPonly_flag_on_cookies: setting this to *0* eliminates access to the session cookie from client scripts, java applets, etc. Although this increases security, it might impact applications using these technologies.
- http/security_session_timeout: the default value is *1800 seconds* or *30 minutes*. Although it eliminates the need for re-authentication, the default value is probably too high for accessing sensitive data as the session remains open for a half an hour, even without any activity from the end user. As such, we recommend you set it to the same value as you would set the timeout of a standard SAP logon session.
- SSO tickets should always be encrypted. Sending tickets in clear text makes them vulnerable to being intercepted and reused. Set profile parameter login/ticket_only_to_host to *1* to make this happen.

Disable sensitive error messages from being sent to the client

Error messages may contain information about host names and IP addresses. A hacker can use this information to figure out your system layout. You can avoid this by setting parameter is/HTTP/show_detailed _errors to *False*. This is recommended by SAP and is the default setting.

Log activities of the Internet Communication Framework

To get an overview of the load on the ICM, you can create an access log via the parameters icm/HTTP/logging_<x> and icm/HTTP/logging_client _<xx>.

4.2 Securing data access

In the end, security is all about protecting the customer, product, material, business, and most importantly, personal data, from unauthorized access. In an SAP context, this translates to protecting the SAP client, auditing data and system access, and securing user logon.

4.2.1 Protecting the SAP client

In the client-server architecture, a *client* is a synonym for an end user, a laptop, or a mobile device. The server is the powerful computer which hosts, manages, and delivers the application. This section is not about the client-server architecture. An SAP client is completely different. It is an entity with an independent set of data. The client concept allows an organization to split the SAP system into logical subunits. When a user connects to an SAP system, he always connects to a client. Once connected, the user can only access data of that client or logical subset.

An SAP system consists of several clients. Every SAP client has customizing, application, and master data and client-dependent data. Some system customizations are shared between all clients. We call these client-independent data. Finally, we have the SAP repository, which consists of the Data Dictionary, programs, transactions, and function modules. These are shared between all clients (see Figure 4.4).

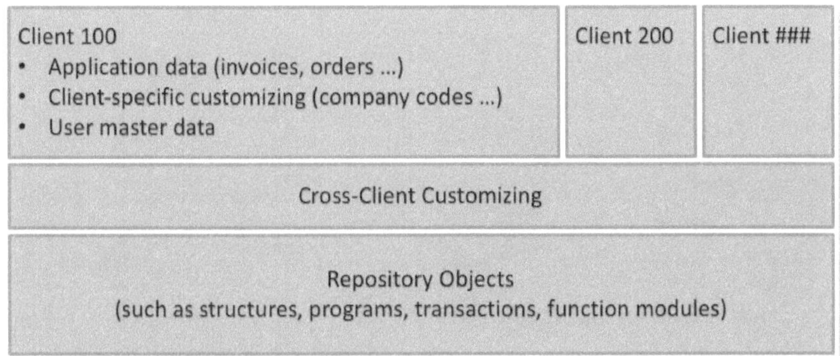

Figure 4.4: SAP client concept and layout

As with everything in SAP, clients have properties which relate to their role in the SAP landscape.

You can set these properties in transaction SCC4 (see Figure 4.5 and Table 4.1):

- CHANGES AND TRANSPORTS FOR CLIENT-SPECIFIC OBJECTS: settings which control whether client-specific objects can be maintained and whether corresponding transports can be executed.
- CROSS-CLIENT OBJECT CHANGES: settings which control how repository and client-independent customizing objects can be changed in the selected client.
- CLIENT COPY AND COMPARISON TOOL PROTECTION: settings which protect the selected client against read access from other clients. When set, tables cannot be compared and the client is protected against being overwritten in the case of a client copy.
- CATT AND ECATT RESTRICTIONS: *CATT* stands for *Computer Aided Test Tool*. CATT is integrated into the SAP ABAP Workbench. *eCATT* is an extension to CATT. Both CATT and eCATT are tools for combining and automating the business process as repeatable test procedures.

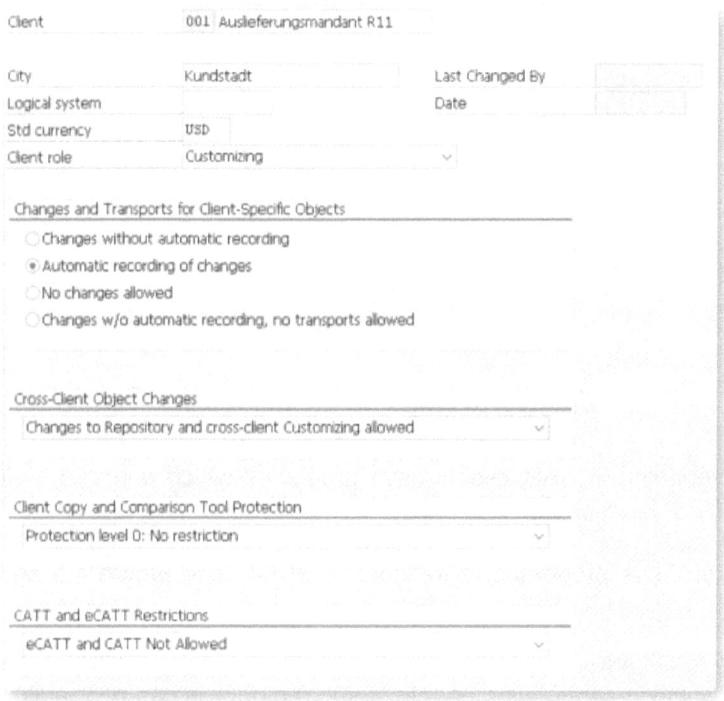

Figure 4.5: Transaction SCC4

Value	Description and recommendations
Changes and Transports for Client-Specific Objects	
Changes without automatic recording	Changes to client-specific customizing can be executed without generating change requests. This option should be used only on sandbox systems whose sole purpose is to allow you to try new functionality which will not be re-used elsewhere.
Automatic recording of changes	This setting is recommended for development systems. Every change is kept in a transport request.
No changes allowed	This setting is recommended for production systems. Changes to client-specific customizing should never be executed on the production system.

Value	Description and recommendations
Changes w/o automatic recording, no transports allowed	Changes are allowed without automatic recording. No manual transport of customizing settings from the client is possible.
Cross-Client Object Changes	
Changes to repository and cross-client customizing allowed	Allow changes to the maintenance of cross-clients objects.
No change to cross-client customizing objects	Disallow the maintenance of cross-client customizing objects in the selected client. This setting is recommended on production systems.
No change to repository objects	Disallow the maintenance of repository objects in the selected client.
No change to repository and cross-client customizing objects	Disallow the maintenance of cross-client customizing or repository objects.
Client Copy and Comparison Tool Protection	
Protection level 0: No restriction	Allow any changes to the client. The selected client may be overwritten by a client copy and any read access from other clients is possible.
Protection level 1: No overwriting	The client cannot be overwritten by a client copy.
Protection level 2: No overwriting, no external availability	The client cannot be overwritten by a client copy. Read access from other clients is not available.
CATT and eCATT Restrictions	
eCATT and CATT Not Allowed	Prevents test scripts being started in the client.
eCATT and CATT Allowed	Enables you to implement eCATT and CATT without restrictions. Using inline ABAP and function modules, any code can be run on the target system (security).

Value	Description and recommendations
eCATT and CATT Only Allowed for 'Trusted RFC'	Automated test cases can be started only if the target system has been addressed via a trusted RFC connection. In this case, the full range of functions can be implemented for tests on this client.
eCATT Allowed, but FUN/ABAP and CATT Not Allowed	Only transactions can be executed in the target client. They must be addressed via eCATT.
eCATT Allowed, but FUN/ABAP and CATT Only for 'Trusted RFC'	This protection level allows function modules to be called and inline ABAP to be executed provided that the connection to the target system is established via a trusted RFC.
Restrictions	
Locked due to client copy	
Protection against SAP upgrade	If you choose this option, then this client will be not updated when an upgrade is implemented. You should use this option for a client that is used for backup purposes or for client 066 (Early Watch client) that is used by SAP for a customer's SAP system performance. If you choose this option for any client, the upgrade will not provide any data to this client and it cannot be used as a regular customizing client.

Table 4.1: Client properties and description

4.2.2 Auditing data changes

SAP data resides in tables. At certain times, it might be useful to track who changed what and when. This is where table logging comes in. The recommendation is to activate logging for tables which are critical or susceptible to audits. Table logging is a very straightforward way of tracking table changes. It can be applied to SAP standard and customer tables.

Table logging can be activated via the parameter rec/client. This parameter specifies whether the SAP system logs table changes in all or only in specific clients.

Table 4.2 shows the possible values for the parameter:

Parameter value	Meaning
Off	Table logging is inactive
All	Table logging is active in all clients
<NUMBER>	Table logging is active in <NUMBER>

Table 4.2: Table logging via parameter rec/client

SAP recommends that you activate table logging only in systems where it is really needed as it impacts performance. It should therefore be used only on production systems. The performance impact should, however, not be overestimated. In addition, the security concern overrules the performance concern in many cases. In SAP HANA systems, the performance impact is negligible.

Setting parameter rec/client is not enough; changes to a specific table will only be logged if:

- The system profile parameter is set to *All*
- The system profile parameter is set to the client in which changes occur

In addition to the parameter setting, automatic recording should be activated on a table-by-table basis via the SAP Workbench.

Proceed as follows to activate or deactivate table change logging:

- Choose TOOLS • ABAP WORKBENCH • DEVELOPMENT • DICTIONARY (transaction SE11) on the initial screen.
- Enter the name of the table whose log settings you want to check.
- Choose CHANGE.
- The table is displayed. The system may ask you for a change key because a change to a Dictionary object is a modification in a customer system. Enter the appropriate data.

- Choose GOTO • TECHNICAL SETTINGS (see Figure 4.6).
- Select/deselect the LOG DATA CHANGES checkbox.
- Select SAVE and ACTIVATE.

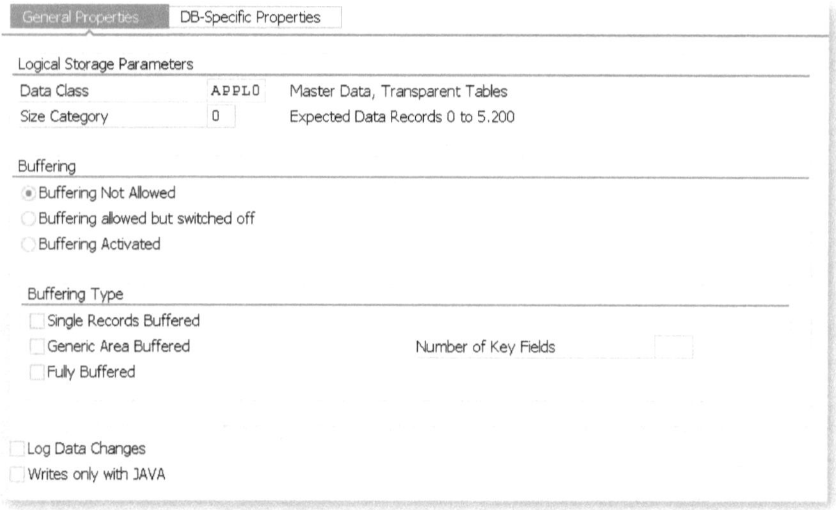

Figure 4.6: Technical settings, logging data changes

To avoid generating too many log entries, deactivate the logging for specific tables when making bulk changes.

Deactivating the logging in the technical settings of the table in the Dictionary is not a modification. You do not have to specify a change key:

- Use transaction SE13 to change technical settings in the Dictionary.
- Enter the table name.
- Choose CHANGE.
- Deselect LOG DATA CHANGES.
- Select ACTIVATE.

How should you manage table logging?

Table changes are logged in table DBTABPRT. You can access the logs via transaction SCU3 and use report RSTBHIST to obtain a list of those tables currently set to be logged. For more information, see SAP Note 1106605 *Setting of parameter rec/client.*

4.2.3 Auditing system access

The *Security Audit Log* was provided with SAP release 4.0, which was released back in 1998. It is one of those things which still exists, does the job quite well, but is unknown by many SAP system administrators. It can be used to record sensitive security-related system information such as changes to user master records and successful and unsuccessful logon attempts.

The tool was developed for auditors who need to take a detailed look at who connects to the SAP system. When activated, activities which you consider important are audited.

Audit logging writes information to audit files. These are available as long as they are not explicitly deleted. As standard storage is cheap, you can keep them as long as needed. You can even move the files to offline storage.

The following activities can be recorded in the audit log:

- Successful and unsuccessful dialog logon attempts
- Successful and unsuccessful RFC logon attempts
- RFC calls to function modules
- Changes to user master records
- Successful and unsuccessful transaction starts
- Changes to the audit configuration

The audit files are located on the individual application servers. You specify the location of the files and their maximum size in the profile parameters rsau/local/file and rsau/max_diskspace_local. You specify the activities that you want to log in filters using transaction SM19. You can read the log using transaction SM20. You can delete old logs with transaction SM18.

Need more information?

The configuration steps and parameters are explained in detail at:

https://help.sap.com/saphelp_nw70/helpdata/en/c7/69bcb7f36611d3a6510000e835363f/frameset.htm

4.2.4 Protecting the standard users

There are several standard or system users which exist in the SAP application server, such as the SAP*, DDIC, and EARLYWATCH users. These users are very vulnerable to hacker attacks as they exist in every SAP system, are well-documented, have extensive authorizations, and worst of all, have default passwords.

Table 4.3 shows the existing standard users:

User	Description	Client	Default password
SAP*	SUPER USER	000, 001, and all new clients	Master password set during installation Hardcoded password SAP* if the user does not exist
DDIC	ABAP dictionary and software logistics user	000, 001	Master password set during installation

User	Description	Client	Default password
EARLY-WATCH	User for the Early Watch service	066	Master password set during installation
SAPCPIC	User for remote connections to legacy systems (4.5B and older)	000, 001, and all new clients	ADMIN
TMSADM	User for the Transport Management System (TMS)	000	Master password set during installation

Table 4.3: Standard users

Please consider the following recommendations for these users:

- SAP* is a special user as it is hardcoded in the system. If the user is deleted, it reverts back to the default authorizations with the default password PASS. This mechanism is well-documented and most attackers are aware of the SAP* user. We recommend that you create an SAP* user with no roles or profiles and lock the account. In addition, it is strongly recommended that you set parameter login/no_automatic_user_sapstar to value *1*. This disables the hardcoded fallback scenario for SAP*. If the user is deleted, the default SAP* with password PASS will not work unless someone is able to change the login parameter and reboot the instance. System administration authorizations are needed to do this. Even if someone succeeds in changing the parameter, bouncing the instance unnoticed is hard to achieve.
- The Data Dictionary user or user DDIC is a user with special authorizations and is used during installations and upgrades. It should not be deleted. You can remove all authorizations from the user, only re-assigning them during an installation or upgrade. The user can also be locked.
- EARLYWATCH is a dialog user used in the service client 066. The default password is SUPPORT. Client 066 is used for EARLY WATCH functions. As of S/4HANA, the client and user are

obsolete and should be removed before the conversion to S/4HANA.

- User SAPCPIC is a legacy user used for communication and it can be deleted. We recommend leaving it and locking it instead.
- The user TMSADM is automatically created when the Change and Transport Management System is set up in client 000. It is used to maintain and administer the transport domain. The password of TMSADM should be changed as the default password is always the same.

Additional recommendations:

- Make sure that you keep an overview of all clients in your system. Pay special attention to empty clients. Remember that the SAP* user reverts to its default in empty clients. To find out which clients you have in your system, use report RSAUDIT_SYSTEM_STATUS in transaction SA38 or start DISPLAY VIEW "CLIENTS": OVERVIEW (transaction SCC4).
- To make sure that the user SAP* has been created in all clients and that the standard passwords have been changed for SAP*, DDIC, SAPCPIC, TMSADM, and EARLYWATCH, use report RSUSR003 (see Figure 4.7).

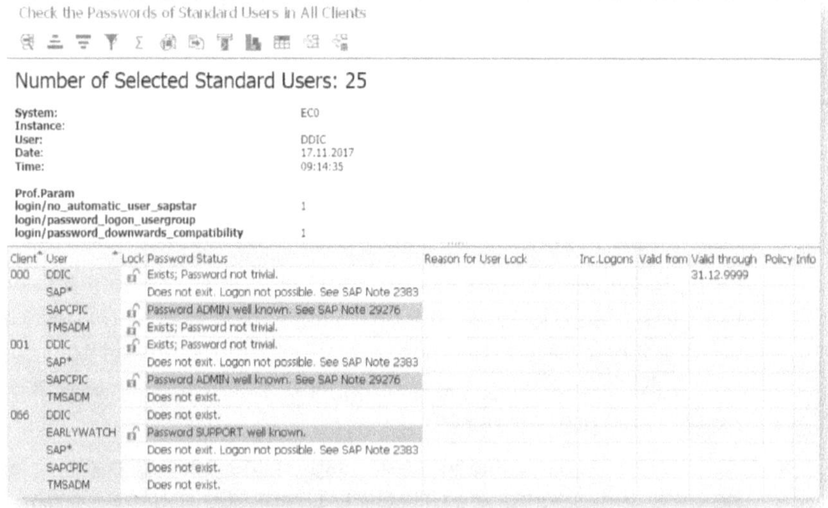

Client	User	Lock	Password Status	Reason for User Lock	Inc.Logons	Valid from	Valid through	Policy Info
000	DDIC		Exists; Password not trivial.				31.12.9999	
	SAP*		Does not exit. Logon not possible. See SAP Note 2383					
	SAPCPIC		Password ADMIN well known. See SAP Note 29276					
	TMSADM		Exists; Password not trivial.					
001	DDIC		Exists; Password not trivial.					
	SAP*		Does not exit. Logon not possible. See SAP Note 2383					
	SAPCPIC		Password ADMIN well known. See SAP Note 29276					
	TMSADM		Does not exist.					
066	DDIC		Does not exist.					
	EARLYWATCH		Password SUPPORT well known.					
	SAP*		Does not exit. Logon not possible. See SAP Note 2383					
	SAPCPIC		Does not exist.					
	TMSADM		Does not exist.					

Figure 4.7: Report RSUSR003

4.2.5 Setting a password policy

Everybody hates passwords—they are either too complicated or too vulnerable to hacker attacks. Many companies are therefore using, or considering using, single-sign-on, especially as end users want access from anywhere from any device. But in the end, even single sign-on requires at least one password. As such, a well-documented password policy is still needed and is always a compromise between security requirements and acceptability by the end user community.

There are many SAP configuration parameters which impact the complexity, length, and validity of passwords:

- Login/min_password_lng: defines the minimum length of a password. The default is six characters but we recommend at least eight. This parameter can be combined with Login/min_passwords_digits = 2, which forces the password to have at least two digits.
- Parameter login/min_passwords_specials specifies the number of special characters required while parameter login/min_password_uppercase specifies the minimum number of upper case characters required. Parameter login/min_passwords_lowercase does the same for lower case characters.
- Setting login/password_compliance_to_current_policy to *1* enables a check that verifies existing passwords against the current password policy. Users with non-compliant passwords will be required to change their password the next time they log on. This parameter should be handled with care. Applying a stricter policy will force all users to change their password the next time they log on. A change like this should be properly communicated to the user community to avoid negative feedback and to avoid users from calling the help desk.
- Setting login/password_max_idle_initial can protect new accounts. If an account is not accessed within a specific amount of time after it is initially created, the account expires. Use this setting to protect against the unauthorized use of inactive accounts.
- The recommendation is to set the login/password_max_idle_productive value to *30*. This parameter specifies the number of days a password remains valid if not used, thereby preventing

hackers taking advantage of inactive user accounts. If the value expires, the user is locked.

- Set login/fails_to_user_lock to *3*. This parameter determines how many times a user can fail to enter a correct password before their account is locked.
- Parameter login/password_hash_algorithm specifies the hash procedure applied when storing passwords in the database. This parameter can be used to overrule the default hash algorithm, which might be used by hackers. See SAP Note 991968 for permissible values.

SAP configuration parameters can be set in the default or the instance profile. The default profile is used for configuration settings which are applicable to the entire SAP system, whereas the instance profile applies to only one instance. It should be clear that password parameters should be set in the default profile to ensure that they are the same on all SAP instances.

Enforce password rules

You can prevent users from choosing passwords which are too obvious, such as the name or address of the company, or easy strings such as 123456 or ABCDEF. To prohibit the use of a password, enter it in table USR40. You can maintain this table via transaction SM30.

Wildcards can be used: *?* stands for a single character, * stands for a sequence of any combination of characters of any length.

Here are some examples:

- 123* prohibits any password that begins with the sequence 123.
- *123* prohibits any password that contains the sequence 123.
- AB? prohibits all passwords that begin with AB and have one additional character: ABA, ABB, ABC, and so on.
- *SAP* prohibits the use of the string SAP in the password.

4.2.6 Securing SAP Logon access

Most users still use SAP GUI to access the SAP system. In those cases, the following security measures should be considered:

- Disable multiple logons via SAP Logon:
  This is a very old security measure which is implemented in many organizations. It avoids multiple logons with the same user ID. Users often share their user name and password because they need something done quickly by a colleague. They know they shouldn't, but they do it anyway because they are getting ready to leave the office or are not even in the office. Accepting this behavior makes it possible for user IDs to be compromised and used to impersonate someone without this being noticed. To disable multiple SAP GUI logons, set the profile parameter login/disable_multi_gui_login to the value *1*.
- Set a timeout to SAP GUI:
  Many end users have the bad habit of leaving their screens open. They are taking a break, are out for lunch, or worse, have gone home. These forgotten sessions are an open door to your SAP system and may be used by an unauthorized user. You can control this by setting the parameter rdisp/gui_auto_logout to a value greater than *0*. This will activate idle GUI session logouts. The related parameter rdisp/keepalive should be set to a value in seconds to define how long GUI sessions should be kept alive.

4.3 Securing SAP Web Dispatcher

SAP Web Dispatcher is a software solution which stands between your SAP system and the Internet. SAP Web Dispatcher is a software firewall and proxy. It is the entry point for HTTP(s) requests to your SAP system. It behaves like a load balancer and will evenly distribute load among the different SAP instances. SAP Web Dispatcher sends queries to the message server (which is part of the ABAP Central Services (ASCS) component) to get the connection details of the application server with the best performance. SAP Web Dispatcher supports many communication scenarios, such as HTTP(s), SSL termination, SSL re-encryption, and X.509 client certificate authentication.

SAP Web Dispatcher is used in Internet-facing scenarios—for example, mobile applications. Allowing access to your SAP system from untrusted networks without protection is not a good strategy. SAP Web Dispatcher should be the first point of entry for all mobile devices (see Figure 4.8). Although the configuration of SAP Web Dispatcher is straightforward, it needs to be hardened as misconfiguration leads to insecurity. In this section, we will list the different configuration steps for securing SAP Web Dispatcher.

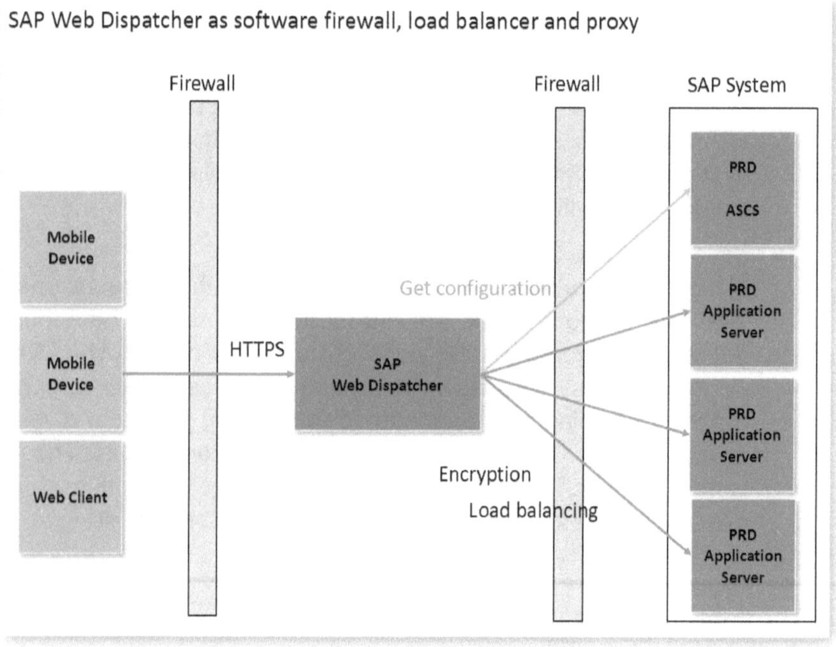

Figure 4.8: SAP Web Dispatcher, architecture overview

The following security measures should be considered in relation to SAP Web Dispatcher. Most of them can be easily implemented.

4.3.1 Update SAP Web Dispatcher regularly

SAP releases new versions of Web Dispatcher regularly, because of new functionality or increased security requirements, for example. The recommendation is therefore to update SAP Web Dispatcher at least twice each year. When installing a new dispatcher, always use the most up-to-date version of SAP Web Dispatcher. SAP Note 538405 describes where you can find the latest version. SAP Web Dispatcher is downwards compatible, which means that the release might be higher or the same as the back-end system.

4.3.2 Use only HTTPS communication

SAP Web Dispatcher can switch HTTP communication to HTTPS automatically. This prevents the use of HTTP communication. The connection via HTTP is re-directed to HTTPS without the user receiving a notification message. HTTPS can also be used between the dispatcher and the back-end system. This can be accomplished via the parameter wdisp/ssl_encrypt.

4.3.3 Implement Web filtering

If you use a URL filter, only positive URLs are allowed to pass through. All the others are blocked. You can define permitted URLs via the parameter wdisp/permission_table. This parameter should point to a file which contains the permitted and denied services.

4.3.4 Disable detailed error logging on SAP Web Dispatcher

Set parameter is/HTTP/show_detailed_errors to *False* to avoid detailed error information being sent to the client. Detailed error logging can disclose sensitive information to hackers, such as host names or IP addresses. Another option is to configure a company error page. A pre-configured error or information page is displayed when an error occurs. This page could describe how to contact the help desk. You can do this via the parameter icm/HTTP/error_templ_path.

4.3.5 Protect administrative access

SAP Web Dispatcher comes with a management tool, accessible via HTTP, in which it can be stopped, re-started, or forced to read the configuration files again. This management tool provides access to the log files. It is obvious that this functionality needs to be protected at all costs.

We therefore strongly recommend the following measures:

- Allow SAP Web Dispatcher to be administered only via ports with a secure protocol (HTTPS) by setting the option PORT for the parameter icm/HTTP/admin_<xx> to an HTTPS port. This port should be accessible only from the internal network.
- Allow administration only using a specific host name/IP address that can be accessed only from the internal network. To do this, use the option HOST for the parameter icm/HTTP/admin_<xx>.
- Use the option CLIENTHOST to restrict access to access only from a trusted client.
- Make sure that anybody connecting to the administrator pages has to supply a password. To do this, use subparameter ALLOWPUB=FALSE of the profile parameter icm/HTTP/admin_<xx>. If ALLOWPUB=FALSE, access to administration pages without having to log on is fully deactivated.

For up-to-date information about security settings for SAP Web Dispatcher, see SAP Note 870127.

4.4 Securing the database

The database is the most important component within an SAP environment. It contains the SAP repository or Data Dictionary, master and customizing data, and all business data. SAP application servers are important for making sure your SAP environment works, but technically they consist of a collection of executable and configuration files. As such, they can be replaced by a new installation or a restore from the last backup easily and quickly. The database cannot be replaced easily and therefore proper disaster recovery procedures must be in place.

As the database contains all business data and logic, it must be protected, as it is a very popular target for intruders. There is a special SAP HANA Security Guide which describes in detail how to protect the SAP HANA database. It also contains recommendations for the underlying infrastructure, for example the operating system, the network, and the storage layer. The guide describes these from a general point of view. For more specific information about the operating system and network, look at the guides from the specific vendors such as the *Operating System Hardening Guide for SAP HANA*, from SUSE.

4.4.1 SAP HANA revisions

As SAP consultants, we are convinced that SAP HANA is great. However, as with all great software, problems will occur and corrections will be needed. These also include security-related improvements, which are released to overcome the exploitation of any weaknesses discovered. SAP publishes information related to security corrections and improvements through SAP security notes. These contain information about the SAP HANA database revisions and application areas that are affected. We recommend that you regularly review security notes and decide whether they are applicable to your environment.

More details on possible update paths from SAP HANA maintenance to standard SAP HANA revisions can be found in SAP Note 1948334. For details about the SAP HANA revision and maintenance strategy, and recommended upgrade paths between SAP HANA revisions, Support Package Stacks, maintenance revisions and data center service points, see SAP Note 2021789 *SAP HANA Revision and Maintenance Strategy*.

4.4.2 Data volume encryption

Data volume encryption is not an SAP HANA technology. It exists in many databases. To protect data saved to disk from unauthorized access at operating system level, the SAP HANA database supports data encryption. Data volume encryption ensures that anyone who can access the data volumes on disk using operating system commands cannot see the actual data. All pages that reside in the data area on disk are encrypted using the AES-256-CBC algorithm. Pages are automatically decrypted as part of the load process into memory. Pages reside in the main memory unencrypted to avoid a performance overhead when accessing them. When changes to data are written back to disk, the relevant pages are automatically encrypted as part of the write operation. As

SAP HANA is an in-memory database, the performance overhead for using data volume encryption is negligible.

Encryption of the database backups is not possible in SAP HANA 1.0. This is unfortunate as database theft is likely to occur via a database backup. A database dump is much smaller than the actual database and is therefore transportable. With SAP HANA 1.0, encryption of the database backup is only possible using third-party tools. Since SAP HANA 2.0 SPS 01, backup encryption is supported natively and can be enabled for all kinds of backup types.

4.4.3 SAP HANA in combination with S/4HANA

SAP HANA in combination with S/4HANA is probably the most straightforward installation option from a user administration perspective. All security-related features, such as authentication, authorizations, business roles, and security auditing are located in the application layer, not in the database. The database is used as a data store only. The application server connects to the database using a technical user. This user or schema owns all the tables of the applications. End users have no direct access to the database. As a consequence, database security is limited to this technical user and any other database administration or operation users which might exist.

This principle is not limited to SAP HANA or even S/4HANA. This is the methodology used by SAP since the release of SAP R/3 back in 1993 in combination with all databases supported by SAP, such as Oracle, Sybase, MaxDB, and SQL-Server.

4.4.4 Database connectivity

The SAP application server connects to the SAP HANA database using the SAP HANA client. The SAP HANA client is deployed on every SAP application server. The SAP installer does this installation automatically.

The application server needs a connection string to connect to the database. The connection string is stored in a secure user store which is part of the SAP HANA client. The secure user store contains the host name and logon credentials of the ABAP schema user in SAP HANA. The secure user store is user specific, so only the operating system user who owns the corresponding secure store file can access the secure store. It is possible, with the appropriate operating system privileges, to manage another user's secure store. This behavior is needed to manage the connection details for ABAP on Microsoft Windows since the application server runs as a service user and not the SAP administrator (SAPService<SAPSID> instead of <SAPSID>adm).

Several measures should be taken to protect the user store. The most obvious is protecting the operating system users who own the secure store. Another additional security measure is the use of the *Secure Storage in File System (AS ABAP) (SSFS)* to store the password of the ABAP database user. This is explained in detail in SAP Notes 1639578 *SSFS as password store for primary database connect* and 2154997 *Migration of hdbuserstore entries to ABAP SSFS*.

4.4.5 SAP HANA multitenant database containers

SAP HANA supports multiple isolated databases in a single SAP HANA system. These are referred to as *multitenant database containers (MDC)*. The multiple database container setup of SAP HANA is comparable to the SQL server or the Sybase ASE instance layout. There is an SAP HANA instance, a system database, and several tenant databases. The system database is used for central system administration. It is also the database from which recoveries of the tenant databases are initiated.

The SAP HANA system installed in multiple-container mode is identified by a single system ID (SID). The HANA SID and a database name identify the databases. From the administration perspective, there is a distinction between tasks performed at system level and those performed at database level. Database clients, such as the SAP HANA Studio, connect to the system or the tenant databases. All the databases in a multiple-container system share the same installation of database system software, the same computing resources, and the same system administration. As a result, software upgrades or system maintenance impacts all databases. Furthermore, system replication applies to the whole SAP HANA instance, thus for all tenant databases including the system database. Newly created tenant databases are integrated into the replication process automatically after they are backed up.

However, each database is fully isolated when it comes to:

- Security: each tenant database has its own users and authorizations which are completely separate from the other tenant databases. The database catalog and repository are also isolated in each tenant database.
- Backups: with SAP HANA multitenant database containers, if each application is deployed on its own tenant database, then each can be backed up and recovered independently.
- Moving and copying tenant databases: tenant databases can be moved or copied using the backup and restore capabilities. This involves downtime only for the tenant database affected. The other tenant databases can stay online. Simply perform a backup, and then either create a new tenant database, restoring the backup into this tenant database; alternatively, restore the copy into an existing tenant database.
- Traces and logs: each tenant database has its own set of trace and log files.

In general, all applications that are supported to run on a single database SAP HANA system are also supported to run on an MDC system. Tools are available for converting a single-container system into a multiple-container system.

Many customers use MDC to consolidate several SAP HANA databases in one SAP HANA system. This setup minimizes the number of appliances and reduces total cost of ownership (TCO).

The system database

A multiple-container system consists of any number of multitenant databases and exactly one system database. The system database is created during the installation or during the conversion of a non-multiple-container system to a multiple-container system. The system database is used for central system administration tasks such as global system configuration settings, the creation of a new tenant database, and system replication. The system database also stores overall system landscape information, including information of the tenant databases. Database information of the tenants, such as the Data Dictionary, is not stored in the system database but in the tenant database catalog.

The SYSTEM user

The SYSTEM user is the database superuser. It is comparable to the SAP* user at the SAP application server level. It has some hardcoded privileges, such as the ability to create other database users, access system tables, and so on. In addition, to ensure that the administration tool SAP HANA cockpit can be used immediately after database creation, SYSTEM is automatically granted several roles the first time the cockpit is opened with this user. In a system with multitenant database containers, the SYSTEM user of the system database has additional privileges for managing tenant databases—for example, creating and dropping databases, changing configuration (*.ini) files of databases, and performing database-specific data backups.

As the SYSTEM user is somehow hardcoded, its existence is well-documented and known by intruders. It is therefore not recommended to use the SYSTEM user for day-to-day activities. Instead, create a dedicated system administrator user and then deactivate the SYSTEM user. You can still use the SYSTEM user as an emergency user even if it has been deactivated. Any user with the system privilege USER ADMIN can reactivate SYSTEM with the statement ALTER USER SYSTEM ACTIVATE USER NOW. It goes without saying that the ALTER USER authority should be assigned sparse privileges and its use should be audited.

Database isolation

Although multiple-database containers share the same SAP HANA installation revision and the same SAP HANA instance, they are isolated from a user, catalog, Data Dictionary repository, and persistence perspective. Backups and restores and database copies can be taken independently. Isolating unauthorized access from an operating system point of view can increase this isolation further. By default, all database processes and files of an SAP HANA system or installation share the same operating system user or <sid>adm user. This implies that if a hacker gets access to the shared <sid>adm user, he gets access to all databases through the operating system. This issue can be tackled by dedicating different operating system users to tenant databases. In this way, the processes of individual tenant databases must run under dedicated operating system users belonging to dedicated operating system groups, instead of all database processes running under <sid>adm. Database-specific data on the file system is subsequently protected using standard operating system file and directory permissions.

More information

For more information on MDC and security, see: *https://help.sap.com/doc/eec734dbb0fd1014a61590fcb5411390/1.0.12/en-US/SAP_HANA_Security_Guide_en.pdf*

SAP HANA services

SAP HANA uses many TCP/UDP ports. Connection to these must be possible for the database to function. The table below contains a list and a short description of all SAP HANA services (see Table 4.4). For more information, please consult the *SAP HANA Master Guide*, Section 2, *The SAP HANA Network*. Most of these ports are dynamically adapted to the instance number of the SAP HANA system. This mechanism ensures that more than one SAP HANA system can be installed on the same system.

Service name	Description	Ports*
HANA_DATABASE_CLIENT	Ports used by client applications	TCP="3xx15 3xx16"
HANA_DATA_PROVISIONING	Connection used for event streaming via SQLDBC (ODBC/JDBC)	TCP="3xx15 3xx17"
HANA_HTTP_CLIENT_ACCESS	Open ports for Web browser client access to SAP HANA	TCP="80xx 43xx"

Service name	Description	Ports*
HANA_SAP_SUPPORT	The connection is not active by default because it is required only in certain support cases; to find out how to open a support connection, see the *SAP HANA Administration Guide*	TCP="3xx09"
HANA_DISTRIBUTED_SYSTEMS	Distributed scenarios: Internal network communication takes place between the hosts of a distributed system on one certified site; SAP HANA hosts contain a separate network interface card that is configured as part of a private network, using separate IP addresses and ports	TCP="3xx00 3xx01 3xx02 3xx03 3xx04 3xx05 3xx07 3xx10 3xx40:3xx99"
HANA_STUDIO	Connection to the SAP HANA instance to allow features such as starting or stopping of the SAP HANA database; the protocol used for this connection is SQLDBC (ODBC/JDBC)	TCP="5xx13 5xx14"

Service name	Description	Ports*
HANA_STUDIO_ LIFECYCLE_MANAGER	This is the connection to SAP HANA lifecycle manager via SAP Host Agent; for more information about SAP HANA lifecycle manager, see *SAP HANA Update and Configuration Guide*; the protocol used for this connection is SQLDBC (ODBC/JDBC)	TCP="1128 1129"
HANA_SYSTEM_ REPLICATION	Distributed scenarios: Internal network communication takes place between the hosts of a distributed system on one certified site; SAP HANA hosts contain a separate network interface card that is configured as part of a private network, using separate IP addresses and ports	TCP="3xy01 3xy02 3xy03 3xy04 3xy05 3xy07 3xy40:3xy99"

Table 4.4: SAP HANA services

* xx = Instance number, for example 00
yy = Instance number + 1

SAP HANA services for multiple-database container systems (MDC)

Every tenant database has its own ports and connections for external and internal communication. These ports are assigned automatically when a tenant database is created. If required in your setup, you can explicitly assign the port numbers to be used when you create the tenant database. The only exception to this is the tenant database that is automatically created when you convert a single-container system to a tenant database system. This database retains the port numbers of the original single-container system.

4.5 Securing the operating system

From a security perspective, the operating system tends to be forgotten. A lot of attention is generally given to the application, the database, and of course, the network. Considering the operating system as impenetrable is a mistake. Many hacker attacks are targeted at the operating system and not the application or database. Once a hacker gains access with sufficient privileges to the operating system, the door is wide open for data theft or worse, total destruction of the system.

4.5.1 Hardening the Linux operating system

The SAP HANA database is available only on Linux. The Linux operating system has many parameters and settings which can improve the overall security of the operating system and its applications and databases.

These settings can be summarized in the following categories:

- Authentication settings:
  Define who is allowed to log on, set password policy, etc.
- System access settings:
  Define which users are allowed to access the system locally and remotely using different logon mechanisms (i.e., local logons via console ttys or remote logons via ssh)
- Service permissions:
  Define the permissions of certain system services, i.e., disabling the 'at' jobs (access to crontab)
- File permissions:
  Define the file access rights of certain security-critical system files
- Logging and reporting:
  Change the behavior of system logging, syslog forwarding to a central syslog server, automatic creation of reports (i.e., security reports) and forwarding of security-relevant information via email

- Network settings:
  Define how certain layers of the network stack behave, i.e., the IP layer or the TCP/UDP layer

Only two builds of Linux are supported by SAP: Linux SUSE Enterprise and Red HAT Enterprise for SAP applications. Both operating systems already provide a high level of security in their standard installation. Some of these settings are generic to fit every possible database or application. SAP HANA is special and does not need or use all features provided by the operating system. As such, a lot of functionality can be switched off without impacting the functionality of SAP HANA. These are documented in the hardening guide which for SUSE, is available at: *https://www.suse.com/documentation/sles11/singlehtml/book_hardening/book_hardening.html*; the hardening guide for Red HAT is available at: *https://access.redhat.com/documentation/en-US/Red_Hat_Enterprise_Linux/7/pdf/Security_Guide/Red_Hat_Enterprise_Linux-7-Security_Guide-en-US.pdf.*

Some general recommendations from the hardening guide:

- Activate the local firewall:
  The local firewall is something which exists in many operating systems such as Windows and SUSE Linux Enterprise. Opening only the network ports on the external interfaces which are used by SAP HANA and any other crucial services enhances operating system security and stability. All other ports remain closed.
- Only install packages used by SAP HANA:
  The fewer operating system packages installed, the fewer the possible security vulnerabilities. Guides exist for SUSE Linux Enterprise and Red Hat Enterprise, describing the packages which are absolutely necessary and packages which can be safely discarded. Another advantage is that the fewer the packages installed, the fewer the number of patches that have to be applied on the system.
- Install security updates and patches:
  Security updates and patches are released regularly. In the case of the Linux operating system, developers, security engineers from the operating system vendors and unfortunately, intruders review the code, constantly looking for vulnerabilities. SUSE and Red Hat provide security updates and patches. A proper implementation and documentation strategy should be in place to install those.

4.5.2 Hardening the Windows operating system

The SAP application server may be installed on Windows. As SAP does not use all the features from Windows, the system can be hardened or closed down, leaving only what is needed by the application. The *Windows Hardening and Patch Management Guide* is available at *https://archive.sap.com/documents/docs/DOC-17123*.

As general recommendations:

- Configure and activate the Windows firewall. Only those ports used by SAP should be allowed to pass.
- Install and configure a Virus scanner. See SAP Note 837594 *Virus scan at SAP* to correctly configure the scanner to avoid a performance impact.
- Only enable services which are really needed. To disable other services, right-click the specific service you have identified and change the startup type to *Disabled*.

4.5.3 The operating system users

Although SAP HANA runs only on Linux, the SAP application servers can run on any operating system supported by SAP, whether it is AIX, HP-Unix, Linux, Oracle Solaris, or Windows. As such, different operating system users exist depending on the operating system family—Unix or Windows.

The following users are created during the installation of the SAP system on Linux and Unix (Table 4.5):

User	Groups	Description
<sid>adm	sapsys, sapinst	SAP system administrator
sapadm	sapsys	SAP Host Agent administrator

Table 4.5: Linux operating system users

The SAP system administrator is used to maintain, start, and stop the SAP application server.

SAP Host Agent is automatically installed when a new SAP system is installed. It is used to monitor the operating system and database. *SAP Landscape Virtualization Management* and the host software lifecycle tools also use it.

SAP Host Agent administrator

Connecting with the sapadm user is rarely necessary. The shell type can therefore be set to */bin/false*.

SAP HANA is restricted to Linux only but the SAP application servers can be installed on Windows. They can be installed in a domain or locally on the Windows server. For more information on the differences between a domain and local installation, refer to the standard Windows documentation. The difference is in the way users are created. In a domain installation, users are stored centrally on the domain controller. This domain controller is accessible to all hosts in the domain. A domain installation is mandatory when you install a distributed SAP system (with several application servers), when you perform a high-availability setup, or when you plan to use a shared transport directory between all SAP systems and those systems run on different computers.

A local installation of SAP application servers should not be considered. Installing all SAP systems on one host is not realistic from a sizing and performance perspective. As such, the transport directory will always need to be shared among the various systems in the SAP landscape.

Table 4.6 lists the users and domain groups, Table 4.7 the local groups on the Windows machine, and Table 4.8 the domain groups.

User	Type	Groups	Description
<sid>adm	Domain user	Local administrators, users, SAP_<SID>_ GlobalAdmin	SAP system administrator
SAPService <SID>	Domain user	Users, SAP_<SID>_ GlobalAdmin	SAP service user; user runs the SAP system
sapadm	Local user	Users, SAP_SAP_ Global Admin	SAP Host Agent administrator

Table 4.6: Users and groups in the Windows domain

Group	Members	Description
SAP_LocalAdmin	SAP_<SID>_ GlobalAdmin	SAP local group for the administrator, SAP services users
SAP_<SID>_LocalAdmin	SAP_<SID>_ GlobalAdmin	SAP local group for the administrator, SAP services users
SAP_SAP_LocalAdmin	sapadm	SAP local group for the SAP Host Agent administrator

Table 4.7: Local Windows groups

Group	Members	Description
SAP_<SID>_GlobalAdmin	<sid>adm, SAPService<SID>	SAP global group for the administrator, SAP services users
SAP_SAP_GlobalAdmin	sapadm	SAP Global group for the SAP Host Agent administrator

Table 4.8: Domain groups

If the users do not exist before the installation, the SAP installer using the master password you supplied during the preparation phase of the installation creates them. This password is used not only for the operating system users but also for the SAP default users, such as SAP* and DDIC. Although the master password has many restrictions, such as its length, forced usage of at least one upper case letter and one number, it is imperative that you change this password after the installation.

4.5.4 The directory structure

SAP stores many files in operating system directories. These should be protected against unauthorized access. Default permissions are set during the installation by the *Software Provisioning Manager*. The values given below are only recommendations—they should be adapted to your security policy. Table 4.9 lists the SAP application server directory structure on Linux and Unix.

Directory	Access rights in octal form	Owner	Group	Description
/usr/sap/<SID>	751	<sid>adm	sapsys	File system of the SAP application server
/usr/sap/<SID>/D < NUMBER>	755	<sid>adm	sapsys	SAP application server directory
/usr/sap/<SID>/D <NUMBER>/sec	700	<sid>adm	sapsys	Directory for the security files
/usr/sap/<SID>/ASCS < NUMBER>	755	<sid>adm	sapsys	SAP ABAP Central Services directory
/usr/sap/<SID>/ERS <NUMBER>	755	<sid>adm	sapsys	SAP enqueue replication server (high-availability installations only)

Directory	Access rights in octal form	Owner	Group	Description
/usr/sap/hostctrl	755	root	sapsys	SAP Host Agent*
/usr/sap/trans	775	<sid>adm	sapsys	Shared directory for the transport directory
/sapmnt/<SID>/global	700	<sid>adm	sapsys	Shared global directory (background jobs, ...)
/sapmnt/<SID>/profile	755	<sid>adm	sapsys	Shared profile directory (instance profiles, default profile)
/sapmnt/<SID>/exe	775	<sid>adm	sapsys	Shared executable directory
<home_directory>/ <sid>adm	700	<sid>adm	sapsys	

Table 4.9: SAP application server directory structure on Linux

The SAP Host Agent directory

Do not change the default permissions for the /usr/sap/hostctrl directory. If you change them, they are automatically reset to their default values the next time SAP Host Agent is started.

Although SAP HANA is an in-memory database, it uses storage for data persistence. Table 4.10 shows the directories used by default:

Directory	Access rights in octal form	Owner	Group	Description
/hana/data	755	<sid>adm	sapsys	Directory for the SAP HANA database
/hana/log	755	<sid>adm	sapsys	Directory for the SAP HANA log
/hana/shared	755	<sid>adm	sapsys	Shared directory, contains the SAP HANA executables, logs files ...

Table 4.10: The default SAP HANA directory structure

UMASK

Newly created files receive access rights as defined in the default UMASK setting. A UMASK is a four-digit octal number which specifies which access rights are going to be given to a newly created file. You can define the default UMASK setting in the following files; login, .cshrc, .profile, or /etc/profile if you want to use the same default UMASK for all users.

The UMASK setting goes from left to right, representing the user, group, and world access. The value of the digit sets the access privilege to be removed (remove none = 0, remove write = 2, remove all = 7). For example, a UMASK of 0027, sets the rights of the newly created file to 750 or read and write for the owner, the group but read-only for others.

See the UNIX documentation for more information on the syntax.

The directory layout is slightly different on Windows (see Table 4.11):

Directory	Group	Access rights	Share	Description
/usr/sap/	SAP_<SID>_GlobalAdmin SAP_<SID>_LocalAdmin SAP_LocalAdmin	All	SAPMNT or SAPLOC	Share SAPMNT is used by the application servers to access the transport directory, shared global, profile and exe directory
/usr/sap/<SID>/SYS	SAP_<SID>_GlobalAdmin SAP_<SID>_LocalAdmin SAP_LocalAdmin	All	N/A	Contains the global, profile, and exe directory
/usr/sap/<SID>/ASCS<NUMBER>	SAP_<SID>_GlobalAdmin SAP_<SID>_LocalAdmin SAP_LocalAdmin	All	N/A	SAP ABAP Central Services directory
/usr/sap/<SID>/D<NUMBER>	SAP_<SID>_GlobalAdmin SAP_<SID>_LocalAdmin SAP_LocalAdmin	All	N/A	SAP application server
/usr/sap/trans	SAP_<SID>_GlobalAdmin SAP_<SID>_LocalAdmin SAP_LocalAdmin	All	N/A	Shared directory for the transport directory

Table 4.11: SAP application server directory structure on Windows

4.5.5 Protecting SAP Management Console

The *Microsoft Management Console (MMC)* is a standard component of Windows. It provides a user interface for system administrators to monitor and maintain their system. The Management Console also provides a common framework for which many third parties have developed add-ons. The advantage of this methodology is that the operating system, database, and application can be managed using the same set of tools, using the same look and feel.

SAP developed the *SAP Management Console* add-on for the Microsoft Management Console (MMC). It allows you to stop and start the SAP application server with a simple mouse click. In addition, it allows you to monitor and perform basic system administration tasks such as:

- Monitoring and controlling (start, stop, or restart) SAP systems (ABAP and Java) and their instances with a single tool
- Displaying and controlling Java and ABAP work processes
- Displaying SAP log and trace files, instance profiles and parameters, the system environment, and SAP landscape
- Monitoring and reviewing system alerts

As of NetWeaver 7.0, SAP Management Console is also available for Unix systems with more or less the same functionality.

If configured incorrectly, access to SAP Management Console is possible without providing user credentials. The default settings are that all activities which change the status of the system are protected (for example, start/stop/restart). However, many other activities can be executed without authentication. These normally pose no risk to the stability of the system but they may reveal information about the SAP landscape and systems which might be exploited elsewhere. It is therefore strongly recommended that you implement the security measures documented in SAP Note 1439348 *Extended security settings for sapstartsrv*.

4.6 Securing the network

Just like many other systems, the SAP system is a client/server application. The network infrastructure is therefore extremely important and should be available at all costs and should be protected from unauthorized access.

Discussing all aspects of network security would be too much for this chapter. Books, even whole libraries have been written on this subject. It is important to remember that S/4HANA is an application and SAP HANA is a database. Network security is no different in an SAP landscape than in any other.

Network security should take the following items into account:

- Layer: limit communication with the SAP system to only what is necessary. All other entry points may be closed down.
- Architecture: use VLANs to keep production systems separate from the non-production systems, to separate server traffic from end user traffic.
- Use firewalls, port restrictions, and package filtering.
- Use a proxy server.
- Disable HTTP access, only accept HTTPS.
- Use network traffic monitoring.

4.6.1 Network ports

For the sake of completeness, the following is a list of the network ports used by the SAP application server and SAP HANA database (see Table 4.12 and Table 4.13).

Ports	Purpose	Notes
36xx	CI/message server	Also used by the Java application server
32xx	SAP Dispatcher	SAP GUI
33xx	SAP Gateway	For CPIC and RFC communication
48xx	SAP Gateway SNC	Secured CPIC and RFC
80xx	ICM HTTP	WebDynpro
81xx	Message server HTTP	Also used by the Java application server
443xx	ICM HTTPs	

Ports	Purpose	Notes
25	ICM SMTP	The SMTP daemon on Unix uses the same port
5xx00	HTTP	
5xx01	HTTPs	

Table 4.12: SAP standard ports for ABAP and Java

Ports	Purpose	Notes
3xx00	SAP HANA database daemon	
3xx01 .. 10	Name server, preprocessor, index server, script server, statistic server, xsengine, compile server	Used for internal communication
3xx15	Index server	External communication
5xx13, 5xx14	Start and stop SAP HANA instances	External communication
1128 & 1129	SAP Host Control	Used for SAP HANA lifecycle management
21212 & 21213	SAP Installation/SAP upgrade	
4238	Upgrade monitor	
3299	SAP router	
3298	Niping	

Table 4.13 SAP standard ports for SAP HANA, SAP Host Control, installation and upgrade tools, and the SAP router

What about the entries in the services file?

There may be many more ports in the services file. The SAP installer creates entries for every possible instance number, regardless of the instance number specified during the installation. For SAP NetWeaver Gateway, for example, entries will exist for sapgw00 or 3300/tcp up to sapgw99 or 3399/tcp.

4.6.2 SAP router

SAP router is a software application that provides remote connections between SAP support and the customer network. It can also be used for connecting SAP systems which do not share the same network, or to allow remote connections of end users to SAP systems for which direct connections are not possible. Connections can be password-protected. They can be limited by means of a permission table. Only connections specified are allowed to pass through. SAP router can even be configured to use SNC encryption. Although SAP router behaves like a firewall, it is not a firewall and should not be seen as a replacement of the network firewall but rather as an extension (see Figure 4.9). SAP router can be used to increase security.

SAP router supports the following scenarios:

- SAP Logon communication to the message server of the SAP application server
- RFC communication to gateway
- Connection for SAP support

SAP router has the following built-in functionalities:

- Security, by forcing encrypted connections
- Access logging the connections to the SAP system
- Setting up indirect connections when programs or users cannot connect to each other due to network configurations or firewall restrictions

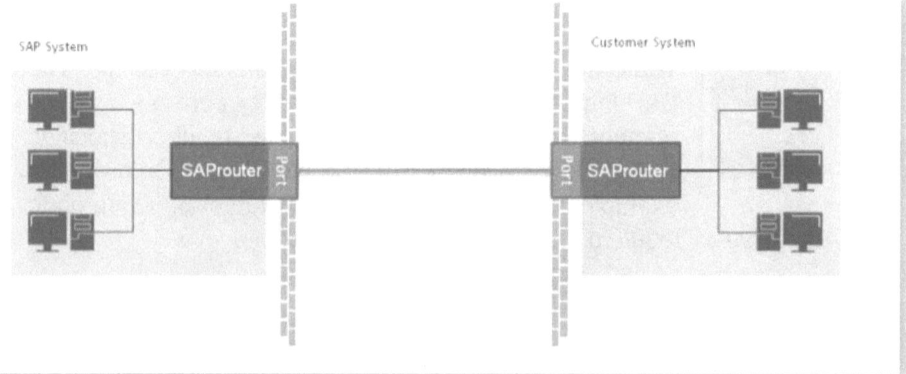

Figure 4.9: SAP router architecture

The SAP router permission table

The SAP router uses a permission table. This table specifies which connections are allowed or prohibited. It contains the hosts and service ports of the predecessor and successor connection ports, as well as any passwords required to set up the connection.

Example entries include:

- P/S/D <source-host> <dest-host> <dest-serv> <password>
- SNC entries for incoming connections have the following syntax: KT <SNCname src-host> <src-host> <src-serv>
- SNC entries for outgoing connections have the following syntax: KT <SNCname dest-host> <dest-host> <dest-serv>
- KP, KS, and KD entries have the following syntax: K<D/P/S> <SNCname source-host> <dest-host> <dest-serv> <password>

The abbreviations above stand for:

- P = Permit the connection
- S = Secure, only NI connections are allowed; NI is the SAP protocol used by SAP programs
- D = Deny, the connection is denied

- KT = The connection must be an SNC connection
- KP = The SNC connection is permitted
- KS = The SNC connection is permitted if it is an NI connection
- KD = The SNC connection is denied

There are many examples of route strings in the SAP documentation. Make sure you always include *D * * ** as the last line in the saprouttab. This string means that all connections are prohibited, except those above the deny string. String *P * * ** is always a bad idea, as it permits all routes from all hosts using all ports and services.

The SAP route table

The SAP route table is always evaluated from top to bottom. If a matching entry is found, the evaluation ends.

Route strings

SAP systems use route strings. A route string describes the connection between two systems or networks through one or more SAP routers. It tells the SAP system how to connect to another system through one or more SAP routers.

A route string has the following syntax:

```
(/H/host/S/service/W/pass)*
```

Where

- `/H/` indicates the host name
- `/S/` is the SAP service or port number; this is optional and the default value is 3299
- `/W/` is the password (optional)

As an example:

```
/H/212.123.12.165/S/sapdp99/H/194.117.106.129/S/sapdp99/H/os
s001
```

This is a connection from an SAP system to SAP support as specified in the RFC connection SAPOSS in the SAP system. The system is to connect to a local host with IP 212.123.12.165 using port 3299 from which it needs to jump to 194.117.106.129 again using 3299. The customer SAP router is running on 212.123.12.165.

Although this connection looks complicated, using transaction OSS1, you can configure the connection in a way that is more understandable to humans. Simply enter transaction OSS1 and select TECHNICAL SETTINGS (see Figure 4.10).

SAProuters at Customer Site

SAProuter 1		SAProuter 2	
Name	VMSAP999	Name	
IP Address	212.123.12.165	IP Address	
Instance no.	99	Instance no.	

SAProuter and SAP Service Marketplace Message Server at SAP

SAProuter at SAP		SAP Service Marketplace Message Srvr	
Name	sapserv3	Name	oss001
IP Address	194.117.106.129	DB Name	001
Instance no.	99	Instance no.	01

SAP GUI for Logging On To SAP Service Marketplace

Current	C:\Program Files (x86)\SAP\FrontEnd\SAPgui\SAPGUI.EXE
Alternative	sapgui

Figure 4.10: Transaction OSS1, technical settings

4.7 Conclusion

Ever since the start of computer technology back in the 1950s, security has been a serious concern. This concern is only going to increase as, according to studies, the quantity of data is going to multiply enormously by 2050. In this chapter, we outlined easy security measures from the top down: from the SAP application server layer, the SAP HANA database, the operating system, and finally the network.

Prevention is better than cure. A mature organization will avoid introducing unnecessary risk by using change management procedures. If these security measures are not yet in place, an implementation plan that considers what is achievable and at what cost must be created. Security is not a one-man show. In many organizations, responsibilities are divided among several teams, such as the database administrators, the operating system and network teams, etc. The implementation plan should take this into account and every team should assign a single point of contact.

For greenfield implementations, securing or hardening the system should be included in the implementation plan from day one. Security tends to be forgotten in greenfield implementations due to lack of time. This is unfortunate, as implementing a thorough security plan takes time and may be difficult in a system that is already running.

Finally, education is important. As you are closing the doors, make the walls higher—intruders are always trying to find new ways to get in.

5 Appendix: References

5.1 SAP Notes

SAP Notes and SAP Knowledge Base Articles (KBA) are support documents that help you find answers to questions arising from your daily work with SAP software products.

We referenced the following SAP Notes:

- 821875: Security settings in the message server
- 1480644: "gw/acl_mode" and "gw/reg_no_conn_info"
- 1444282: gw/reg_no_conn_info settings
- 1989587: GW: Interface for maintenance of gateway security files
- 2325191: GW: Maintenance of gateway ACL files
- 161146: RFC logon with the initial password
- 1106605: Setting of parameter rec/client
- 991968: List of values for "login/password_hash_algorithm"
- 538405: SAP Web Dispatcher: composite note
- 870127: Security note for SAP Web Dispatcher
- 1948334: SAP HANA Database Update Paths for SAP HANA Maintenance Revisions
- 2021789: SAP HANA 1.0 Revision and Maintenance Strategy
- 2378962: SAP HANA 2.0 Revision and Maintenance Strategy
- 1639578: SSFS as password store for primary database connect
- 2154997: Migration of hdbuserstore entries to ABAP SSFS
- 837594: Virusscan@SAP
- 1439348: Extended security settings for sapstartsrv

5.2 Articles and other publications

In addition to the SAP Notes, we used the following documentation and white papers:

From SAP:

- SAP HANA Platform 2.0: Master Guide
- SAP HANA Platform 2.0: Security Guide
- SAP HANA Platform 2.0: Administration Guide

From other parties:

- Operating System Security Hardening Guide for SAP HANA, Developed for SAP HANA Running on SUSE Linux Enterprise Server
- SUSE Linux Enterprise Server for SAP Applications 12 SP3
- SUSE Linux Enterprise Server 11.x for SAP Applications Configuration Guide for SAP HANA
- Red Hat Enterprise Linux (RHEL) 7.x Configuration Guide for SAP HANA
- SAP Hardening and Patch Management Guide for Windows Server

You have finished the book.

A The Authors

Christophe Decamps

Christophe is a GRC Senior Consultant at Expertum. With seven years of experience in SAP security, Christophe has performed several implementations and access reviews and provided support for the SAP authorizations concept. Over the years, Christophe has focused on the next generation of SAP authorizations: SAP Fiori and HANA. He has held multiple training courses and presentations on those topics, including at SAPinsider events.

He can be contacted at christophe.decamps@expertum.net.

Bert Vanstechelman

Bert Vanstechelman is a partner of and principal technical consultant at Expertum. He has more than 20 years of experience in SAP technical consulting, covering all kinds of SAP versions in combination with all possible databases and operating systems supported by SAP. Bert specializes in platform migrations, SAP release upgrades, and SAP HANA conversions. Bert is the founder of Logos Consulting, now part of Expertum.

Bert is a member of the board of advisors of the SAP Professional Journal. He is the author of the SAP HANA Implementation Guide published by Espresso Tutorials. He is also the co-author, with Mark Mergaerts, of the following SAP PRESS books: Upgrading SAP, SAP NetWeaver Application Server Upgrade Guide, The OS/DB Migration Project Guide, and the mySAP ERP Upgrade Project Guide.

He can be contacted at bert.vanstechelman@expertum.net.

Chris Walravens

Chris Walravens is a partner of and GRC Community Lead at Expertum. Chris became an SAP security and GRC consultant in 2000 after having worked as an IT auditor and after qualifying as a Certified Information Systems Auditor. He specializes in designing, implementing, and supporting logical access architectures adapted to your business and to your SAP landscape, combining technical SAP skills with extensive knowledge of audit, internal controls, and business processes. Chris also focuses on setting up adequate monitoring and auditing procedures, using state-of-the-art GRC applications available on the market. His multidisciplinary knowledge puts him in an ideal position to understand security business requirements, to translate them into a transparent authorizations setup, and to integrate audit and compliance requirements and internal controls principles into an overall security and internal controls architecture.

He can be contacted at chris.walravens@expertum.net.

About Expertum

The Expertum team consists entirely of consultants with long and extensive experience in SAP technology.

Expertum offers functional and technical expertise in a broad range of SAP solutions, from S/4HANA, Hybris, Analytics to SAP Security, Solution Manager, etc. It also offers the technological know-how on how to best install, migrate, upgrade, integrate, monitor, and maintain these SAP solutions and underlying databases.

Our mission is to provide in-depth technical and functional expertise in the SAP area: to assist our customers and our implementation partners during their key projects and daily operations. We aim to establish long-term relationships in order to assist our customers today and to continue to provide them with future-proof strategic platform and solution advice for tomorrow.

Our consultants are our most important assets. We inspire them to be the best and provide them with the necessary support, education, and knowledge sharing to do so. This approach provides our customers with focused and motivated individuals who act as trusted advisors.

We strive for continuing relationships in which we guide our customers during periods of high workload. We assist them in large implementation projects—with assignments ranging from full-time on-site presence up to frequent visits. Remote support, to take the daily administration burden out of our customers' hands, can also be provided. Finally, in emergency situations, our consultants go the extra mile to ensure a quick recovery of system infrastructure.

We strongly believe in the exchange of knowledge and information to the benefit of our consultants and our partners. In co-operation with Espresso Tutorials, we published *The SAP HANA Implementation Guide* and with SAP PRESS, we have published the following SAP books:

- Upgrading SAP
- SAP NetWeaver Application Server Upgrade Guide
- ERP Upgrade Project Guide
- The SAP OS/DB Migration Project Guide

Furthermore, we advise the SAP Professional Journal on technical SAP subjects.

Expertum goes SAP HANA

From 2025, SAP solutions will be supported only on SAP HANA. Several SAP solutions are today already available only on SAP HANA—for example, S/4HANA.

Expertum is the leader in SAP HANA implementation projects in Belgium and the quality and experience of our certified consultants are widely acknowledged. This was recognized by SAP Belgium when they awarded Expertum the SAP HANA innovation award in 2014, when they joined forces with Expertum during the **SAP HANA in the Box** campaign in 2015, and when they recently awarded Expertum the SAP Quality Award for the fast delivery implementation for BW on HANA in 2017.

About SUSAN

The Susan Smart platform (see Figure 5.1) is a comprehensive system for monitoring all aspects of SAP NetWeaver ABAP and SAP NetWeaver Java systems. Susan Smart has been developed by Expertum and builds on the company's extensive expertise in the field of SAP technology.

Expertum uses SAP Solution Manager, which covers a very wide range of SAP solutions, as a foundation for monitoring and supporting customer systems. However, we made the conscious decision that for SAP NetWeaver systems, which are at the very heart of a company's SAP landscape, we needed more than what Solution Manager provides. Leveraging the extensive experience and in-depth knowledge of Expertum consultants has resulted in the unique power and flexibility of Susan Smart.

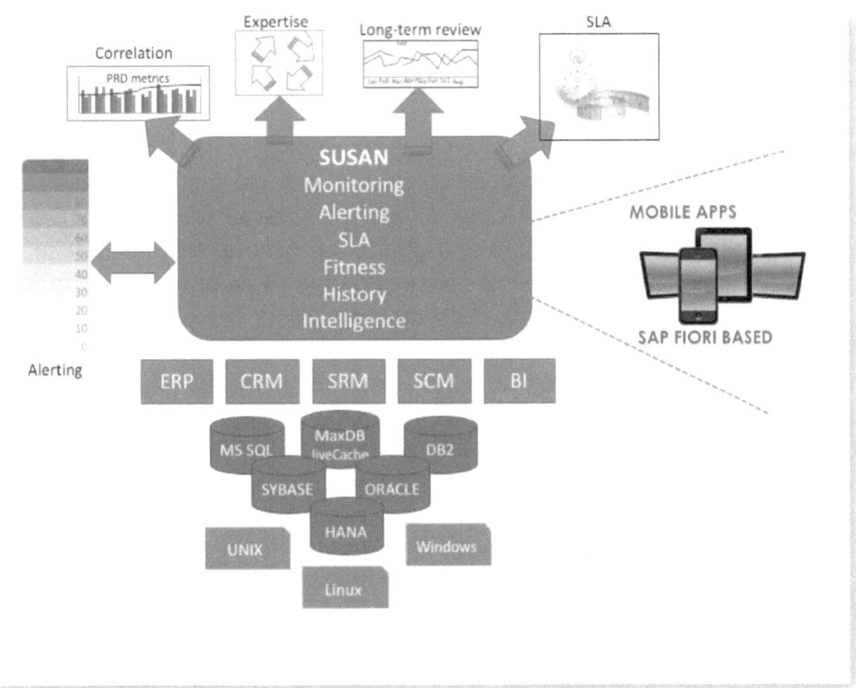

Figure 5.1: Susan Smart platform

Data collection and alerts

Susan Smart monitors the SAP NetWeaver system using a data collection process that is powerful and highly flexible but has itself a very small footprint. Elements are monitored at (configurable) frequencies that take into account their criticality and their likelihood to change at short notice, with the ability to check crucial KPIs as often as once per minute.

Susan Smart goes beyond the traditional traffic light metaphor, where a monitored element is simply flagged as green (OK), yellow (warning), or red (problem). Experience shows that this is too crude a method for evaluating the status of a system, especially if, as is the case for the SAP NetWeaver system, the number of monitored elements is large. Instead of the rudimentary red-yellow-green differentiation, Susan Smart uses a sophisticated *color calculus* which takes into account not only the seriousness of the alert, but also other things such as the context in which the alert is occurring. This ensures that the status of the system is diagnosed in a fine-grained manner and avoids issues such as *red saturation* where, at any one time, numerous elements are reported with a red status.

Alerts can trigger the automatic creation of a ticket in the support system (Expertum's own support desk is fully integrated with Susan Smart). They can also be configured to trigger other actions such as sending an email or transmitting a text or voice message to an on-call support engineer. Other information channels into which Susan feeds its information are the *kiosk* (the equivalent of the alert inbox in other products), a dashboard showing the status of a system or group of systems at a glance, and a collection of graphs and statistical reports.

Reporting

Monitoring with Susan Smart does more than trigger alerts. The information collected is used to build an extensive knowledge database, which in turn serves as the basis for a set of convenient reports. The collector configuration is so flexible that you can set the frequency of each collector to as low as one minute or as high as days or weeks. This enables you to set up a monitoring schedule that constantly keeps a close eye on the SAP NetWeaver system while at the same time relieving administrators of repetitive work. Here are some examples:

- The *Early Morning Report*: system administrators often verify the system every morning through time-consuming and error-prone *transaction hopping*, executing transactions such as SM37, SM58, SMQR, SMQS, SM12, SM13, SM50, SM51, SM66, ST22, WE05, and many more. Susan Smart automates this tedious chore by automatically generating its Early Morning Report, which is ready and waiting for the administrator at the start of the workday. Users can navigate through earlier reports up to 14 days old to examine how an issue has evolved over time.
- Hourly reporting: to follow the system status by the hour, Susan Smart generates an hourly update from a full system monitoring report. The hourly updates are then made available in a time-navigable interface. Navigation through earlier reports, up to 48 hours old, is possible.

- In update mode, the hourly reports are continuously updated as new data from the collectors becomes available, which makes even the reporting facility seem real-time.
- High frequency monitoring: because of Susan Smart's ability to run collectors as often as every minute, it can keep a permanent watch on critical elements of the system. This results in an **immediate response**, making any event of interest appear in the kiosk or on the dashboard, generating a support incident, and showing up in the reports.

In addition to its monitoring functions, Susan Smart is also capable of generating a detailed system review over any requested time period (weeks, months, or even years).

Customization

The design of the Susan Smart collection process makes it very easy to add or enhance data collectors. Our customers have frequently benefited from this capability because we have been able to provide them with alerts within just a few days; with other products, this would have taken months or would never have been developed at all due to the specificity of the request. Two real-life examples to illustrate this:

- An Expertum customer wanted a specific alert (and the possibility to report) for short dumps that originated in code developed in-house (Z programs). This feature was helpful with a quality review of their internal development.
- Another customer wanted a high-level alert and a customized text message if a specific background job did not run or started later than a certain cut-off time. This was a critical job for vehicle planning and thanks to the custom alert, the business process could be made more robust.

Installation and configuration

In contrast to SAP Solution Manager and most third-party monitoring products, Susan Smart is extremely easy to install and maintain. The data collection uses standard functions in SAP as much as possible.

Where standard functions are not available, Susan Smart uses a light-weight agent installed in the monitored system; this is the only software to be installed there.

Thanks to its efficient, performance-oriented design, Susan Smart has the capacity to monitor dozens or even hundreds of systems simultaneously. A new system can be added to the Susan Smart watch list in a matter of minutes.

B Index

S

T

U

W

C Disclaimer

This publication contains references to the products of SAP SE.

SAP, R/3, SAP NetWeaver, Duet, PartnerEdge, ByDesign, SAP BusinessObjects Explorer, StreamWork, and other SAP products and services mentioned herein as well as their respective logos are trademarks or registered trademarks of SAP SE in Germany and other countries.

Business Objects and the Business Objects logo, BusinessObjects, Crystal Reports, Crystal Decisions, Web Intelligence, Xcelsius, and other Business Objects products and services mentioned herein as well as their respective logos are trademarks or registered trademarks of Business Objects Software Ltd. Business Objects is an SAP company.

Sybase and Adaptive Server, iAnywhere, Sybase 365, SQL Anywhere, and other Sybase products and services mentioned herein as well as their respective logos are trademarks or registered trademarks of Sybase, Inc. Sybase is an SAP company.

SAP SE is neither the author nor the publisher of this publication and is not responsible for its content. SAP Group shall not be liable for errors or omissions with respect to the materials. The only warranties for SAP Group products and services are those that are set forth in the express warranty statements accompanying such products and services, if any. Nothing herein should be construed as constituting an additional warranty.

More Espresso Tutorials Books

Tracy Juran

Beginner's Guide to SAP® Security and Authorizations

- Basic architecture of SAP Security and Authorizations
- GRC Access Control introduction
- User profile creation and role assignments
- Common security and authorization pain point troubleshooting

http://5013.espresso-tutorials.com

Christian Savelli:

SAP® BW on SAP HANA

- Tips for upgrading, maintaining, and running BW on HANA
- Data loading methods and real-time data acquisition
- New reporting paradigm for BW on HANA
- HANA data architecture

http://5128.espresso-tutorials.com

Janet Salmon & Claus Wild:

First Steps in SAP® S/4HANA Finance

- Understand the basics of SAP S/4HANA Finance
- Explore the new architecture, configuration options, and SAP Fiori
- Examine SAP S/4HANA Finance migration steps
- Assess the impact on business processes

http://5149.espresso-tutorials.com

Raquel Seville:

SAP® OpenUI5 for Mobile BI and Analytics

- Delve into the foundations of CSS, HTML5, and jQuery
- Learn how to build a seamless mobile BI app using SAP OpenUI5
- Use open source library d3.js to create custom data visualizations for bar, line, and pie charts
- Build web apps using real world scenarios and test layout options for different mobile devices

http://5173.espresso-tutorials.com

Robert Burdwell:

First Steps for Building SAP®UI5 Mobile Apps

- Introduction to mobile and SAP UI5 development
- Steps for building mobile apps in Eclipse, SAP Cloud Platform, and Microsoft Visual Studio
- How to deploy apps to multiple devices
- Advantages and disadvantages of using different environments

http://5176.espresso-tutorials.com

Frank Riesner, Klaus-Peter Sauer:

SAP® BW/4HANA and BW on HANA

- Migration, sizing, operation, data management with SAP BW/4HANA and SAP BW 7.5 on HANA
- The new central source Systems SAP HANA and ODP
- New modeling options, mixed scenarios, LSA++, and differences compared to SAP BW 7.5
- The role of BW in operational SAP reporting

http://5215.espresso-tutorials.com

Maxim Chuprunov:

Leveraging SAP® GRC in the Fight Against Corruption and Fraud

- Overview of classic SAP ABAP interface techniques
- Design and implement an anti-corruption initiative
- Automated drivers and added value GRC
- Detection scenarios using SAP Fraud Management and SAP HANA

http://5216.espresso-tutorials.com/

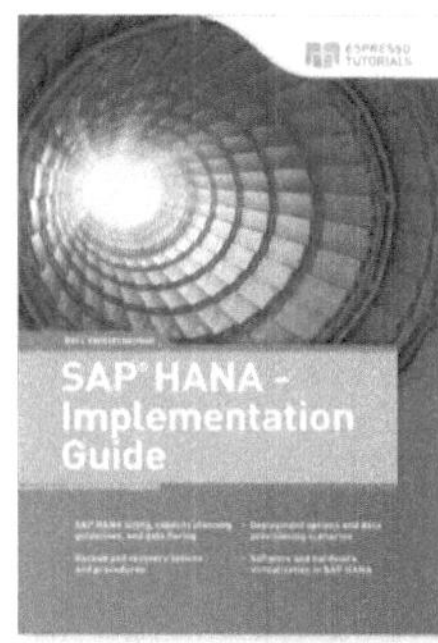

Bert Vanstechelman:

The SAP® HANA Implementation Guide

- SAP HANA sizing, capacity planning guidelines, and data tiering
- Deployment options and data provisioning scenarios
- Backup and recovery options and procedures
- Software and hardware virtualization in SAP HANA

http://5289.espresso-tutorials.com

www.ingramcontent.com/pod-product-compliance
Lightning Source LLC
LaVergne TN
LVHW042320190726
843491LV00018B/224

9783960122494